LITERATURE MADE EASY

WILLIAM SHAKESPEARE'S

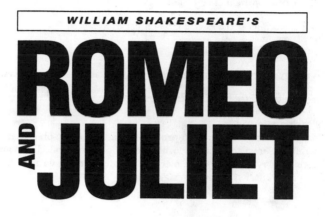

ROMEO AND JULIET

Written by LISA FABRY

WITH TONY BUZAN

BARRON'S

First edition for the United States and Canada published by Barron's Educational Series, Inc., 1999

Copyright © 1999 U.S. version, Barron's Educational Series, Inc.

First published in the United Kingdom by Hodder & Stoughton Ltd. under the title: *Teach Yourself Literature Guides: A Guide to Romeo & Juliet*

Copyright © 1998 Lisa Fabry
Introduction Copyright © 1998 Tony Buzan

Cover photograph © The Ronald Grant Archive
Mind Maps: Anne Jones
Illustrations: Karen Donnelly

Lisa Fabry asserts the moral right to be identified as the author of this work.

American text edited by Elizabeth Schmid

All inquiries should be addressed to:
Barron's Educational Series, Inc.
250 Wireless Boulevard
Hauppauge, New York 11788
http://www.barronseduc.com

International Standard Book No. 0-7641-0832-8
Library of Congress Catalog Card No. 98-73261

PRINTED IN THE UNITED STATES OF AMERICA
987654321

CONTENTS

Important Note to Students About Line References

Line references are to The New Folger Library edition of Shakespeare's *Romeo & Juliet*. If you have another edition, the line numbers may vary slightly from those provided in this book, although the act and scene numbers should be the same. The line references from the New Folger edition have been provided to help direct you to specific parts of the play, but often will not be an exact match for line numbers in other editions.

HOW TO STUDY

There are four important things you must know about your brain and memory to revolutionize the way you study:

♦ how your memory ("recall") works *while* you are learning
♦ how your memory works *after* you have finished learning
♦ how to use Mind Maps – a special technique for helping you with all aspects of your studies
♦ how to prepare for tests and exams.

Recall during learning
– THE NEED FOR BREAKS

When you are studying, your memory can concentrate, understand, and remember well for between 20 and 45 minutes at a time, then it needs a break. If you continue for longer than this without a break, your memory starts to break down. If you study for hours nonstop, you will remember only a small fraction of what you have been trying to learn, and you will have wasted hours of valuable time.

So, ideally, *study for less than an hour*, then take a five- to ten-minute break. During the break listen to music, go for a walk, do some exercise, or just daydream. (Daydreaming is a necessary brain-power booster – geniuses do it regularly.) During the break your brain will be sorting out what it has been learning, and you will go back to your books with the new information safely stored and organized in your memory. We recommend breaks at regular intervals as you work through this book. Make sure you take them!

v

Recall after learning
— THE WAVES OF YOUR MEMORY

What do you think begins to happen to your memory right after you have finished learning something? Does it immediately start forgetting? No! Your brain actually *increases* its power and continues remembering. For a short time after your study session, your brain integrates the information, making a more complete picture of everything it has just learned. Only then does the rapid decline in memory begin, and as much as 80 percent of what you have learned can be forgotten in a day.

However, if you catch the top of the wave of your memory, and briefly review (look back over) what you have been studying at the correct time, the memory is imprinted far more strongly, and stays at the crest of the wave for a much longer time. To maximize your brain's power to remember, take a few minutes at the end of a day and use a Mind Map to review what you have learned. Then review it at the end of a week, again at the end of a month, and finally a week before your test or exam. That way you'll ride your memory wave all the way there – and beyond!

The Mind Map ®
— A PICTURE OF THE WAY YOU THINK

Do you like taking notes? More important, do you like having to go back over and learn them before tests or exams? Most students I know certainly do not! And how do you take your notes? Most people take notes on lined paper, using blue or black ink. The result, visually, is boring. And what does *your* brain do when it is bored? It turns off, tunes out, and goes to sleep! Add a dash of color, rhythm, imagination, and the whole note-taking process becomes much more fun, uses more of your brain's abilities, and improves your recall and understanding.

Generally, your Mind Map is highly personal and need not be understandable to any other person. It mirrors *your* brain. Its purpose is to build up your "memory muscle" by creating images that will help you recall instantly the most important points about the characters and plot sequences in a work of fiction you are studying.

You will find Mind Maps throughout this book. Study them, add some color, personalize them, and then try drawing your own – you'll remember them far better. Stick them in your files and on your walls for a quick-and-easy review of the topic.

HOW TO DRAW A MIND MAP

1 First of all, briefly examine the Mind Maps and Mini Mind Maps used in this book. What are the common characteristics? All of them use small pictures or symbols, with words branching out from the illustration.
2 Decide which idea or character in the book you want to illustrate and draw a picture, starting in the middle of the page so that you have plenty of room to branch out. Remember that no one expects a young Rembrandt or Picasso here; artistic ability is not as important as creating an image you (and you alone) will remember. A round smiling (or sad) face might work as well in your memory as a finished portrait. Use marking pens of different colors to make your Mind Map as vivid and memorable as possible.
3 As your thoughts flow freely, add descriptive works and other ideas on the colored branching lines that connect to the central image. Print clearly, using one word per line if possible.
4 Further refine your thinking by adding smaller branching lines, containing less important facts and ideas, to the main points.
5 Presto! You have a personal outline of your thoughts about the character and plot. It's not a stodgy formal outline, but a colorful image that will stick in your mind, it is hoped, throughout classroom discussions and final exams.

HOW TO READ A MIND MAP

1 Begin in the center, the focus of your topic.
2 The words/images attached to the center are like chapter headings; read them next.
3 Always read out from the center, in every direction (even on the left-hand side, where you will have to read from right to left, instead of the usual left to right).

USING MIND MAPS

Mind Maps are a versatile tool; use them for taking notes in class or from books, for solving problems, for brainstorming with friends, and for reviewing and working for tests or exams – their uses are endless. You will find them invaluable for planning essays for coursework and exams. Number your main branches in the order in which you want to use them and off you go – the main headings for your essay are done and all your ideas are logically organized.

Preparing for tests and exams

◆ Review your work systematically. Study hard at the beginning of your course, not the end, and avoid "exam panic."
◆ Use Mind Maps throughout your course, and build a Master Mind Map for each subject – a giant Mind Map that summarizes everything you know about the subject.
◆ Use memory techniques such as mnemonics (verses or systems for remembering such things as dates and events).
◆ Get together with one or two friends to study, compare Mind Maps, and discuss topics.

AND FINALLY...

Have *fun* while you learn – it has been shown that students who make their studies enjoyable understand and remember everything better and get the highest grades. I wish you and your brain every success! (Tony Buzan)

HOW TO USE THIS GUIDE

This guide assumes that you have already read *Romeo & Juliet*, although you could read Background and The Story of *Romeo & Juliet* before that. It is best to use the guide alongside the play. You could read the Who's Who? and Themes and Imagery sections without referring to the play, but you will get more out of these sections if you do refer to it to check the points made in these sections, and especially when thinking about the questions designed to test your recall and help you think about the play.

THE DIFFERENT SECTIONS

The Commentary section can be used in a number of ways. One way is to read a scene in the play, and then read the Commentary for that scene. Continue until you come to a test section, test yourself – then take a break. Or, read the Commentary for a scene, then read the scene in the play, then go back to the Commentary. Find out what works best for you.

Topics for Discussion and Brainstorming gives topics that could well appear on exams or provide the basis for coursework. It would be particularly useful for you to discuss them with friends, or brainstorm them using Mind Map techniques (see p. vi).

How to Get an "A" in English Literature explains what to look for in a novel or play, and what skills you need to develop to achieve a lifelong appreciation of literature.

The Exam Essay is a useful night-before reminder of how to tackle exam questions, and Model Answer and Essay Plan gives an example of an "A"-grade essay and the Mind Map plan used to write it.

THE QUESTIONS

Whenever you come across a question in the guide with a star ✪ in front of it, think about it for a moment. You could even jot down a few words to focus your mind. There is not usually a "right" answer to these questions; it is important for you to develop your own opinions. The Test Yourself sections are designed to take you about 10–20 minutes each – which will be time well spent. Take a short break after each one.

Key to icons

THEMES

A **theme** is an idea explored by an author. Whenever a theme is dealt with in the guide, the appropriate icon is used. This means you can find where a theme is mentioned just by flicking through the book. Try it now.

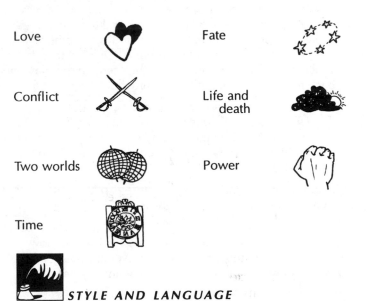

Love

Fate

Conflict

Life and death

Two worlds

Power

Time

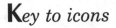 **STYLE AND LANGUAGE**

This heading and icon are used in the Commentary wherever there is a special section on the author's choice of words and imagery.

Romeo and Juliet is a tragedy written in the early part of Shakespeare's career, probably about the same time as the comedy, *A Midsummer Night's Dream*. No one can be sure exactly when Shakespeare's plays were written, but as *Romeo and Juliet* was published in 1597, it must have been written before then. The idea for the play is not original. Several writers in Italy, France, and England, earlier in the century, refer to a story of two young lovers from opposing families. Shakespeare based his play most closely on a long poem by Arthur Brooke, *The Tragical History of Romeus and Juliet*, which was written in 1562. Brooke said his story was about:

> ... a couple of unfortunate lovers, thralling themselves to unhonest desire, neglecting the authority and advice of parents and friends, conferring their principal counsels with drunken gossips and superstitious friars, attempting all adventures of peril, for the attaining of their wished lust, abusing the honourable name of lawful marriage to cloak the shame of stolen contracts, finally by all means of an honest life, hastening to most unhappy death.

Shakespeare's adaptation

Shakespeare is more sympathetic to his Romeo and Juliet. He changes Brooke's story by compressing the action from nine months into five days, making Juliet two years younger, adding the character of Mercutio, and giving life to the other characters in the play. While Brooke's poetry is rather flat and unimaginative, Shakespeare's language brings the story to life, making each character distinctive and memorable, revealing the turmoil of emotions experienced by Romeo and Juliet, and evoking moods of violence, tenderness, humor, passion, and terror.

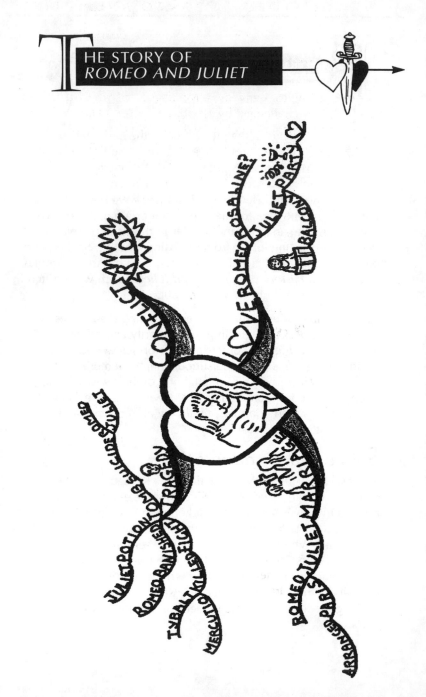

Act 1

A fight breaks out between servants of the Capulet and Montague families. Benvolio, a Montague, tries to stop the fight but he is challenged by Tybalt, a Capulet. Others join in and soon there is a riot going on. Prince Escalus arrives and calls a halt to the fighting. Complaining that the feud between the families has resulted in three such brawls, he declares that anyone caught fighting in the streets again will be executed.

Lord and Lady Montague are worried about their son Romeo. They ask Benvolio to find out what is wrong. Romeo tells Benvolio that he is in love with a woman who has sworn to remain chaste. Benvolio advises him to forget her.

Paris wants to marry Lord Capulet's daughter Juliet. Capulet says that she is too young but promises that if Paris can win her love, he will approve of the marriage. He invites Paris to a party that he is having that evening and sends a servant out with an invitation list. When the servant asks Benvolio and Romeo to help him read the list, Romeo discovers that the woman he loves, Rosaline, will be at the party. Even though no Montagues are invited, Romeo and Benvolio decide to go.

Lady Capulet asks Juliet if she would like to marry Paris. Juliet says she will be happy to meet him at the party and see if she likes him. The Nurse is excited that Juliet might marry such a handsome gentleman.

Romeo, Benvolio, and Mercutio decide to gate-crash the Capulet party by wearing masks. Romeo is depressed about Rosaline, and Mercutio tries to cheer him up. At the party, Romeo spots Juliet across the crowded room and falls in love at first sight. Tybalt recognizes Romeo's voice and threatens to kill him, but Lord Capulet orders him to leave Romeo alone. Romeo and Juliet meet and kiss. Afterwards, they discover that they are the children of bitter enemies.

Act 2

Later that night, Romeo climbs into the Capulet garden and sees Juliet at her window. They exchange vows of love and Juliet asks Romeo to arrange for them to get married. Romeo visits Friar Lawrence, who promises to marry them in the hope that it will end the feud. With the Nurse's help, they are married that afternoon.

Act 3

Tybalt, furious at Romeo for gate-crashing the Capulet party, comes looking for him. Romeo is now related to Tybalt by marriage, and so refuses to fight him. Mercutio fights Tybalt instead and is killed. Romeo kills Tybalt in revenge and is banished from Verona. Romeo and Juliet are both devastated, but the Friar thinks of a plan to help them. Romeo will go to Mantua. After a while, the Friar will tell everyone about their marriage, ask the Prince's forgiveness, and reconcile the two families.

Romeo and Juliet spend one night together. In the meantime, Lord Capulet promises Paris that Juliet will marry him and arranges the wedding for Thursday. He asks Lady Capulet to tell Juliet.

Dawn comes and Romeo and Juliet part. Romeo leaves for Mantua, narrowly missing Lady Capulet, who has come to tell Juliet about Lord Capulet's decision. Juliet refuses to marry Paris and her father threatens to turn her out of his house if she does not.

Act 4

Juliet goes to the Friar, who thinks of a second plan. Juliet must agree to marry Paris. The night before the wedding, she must take a potion that will make it look as if she is dead. Her family will place her in the tomb. Juliet will wake up 42 hours later. In the meantime, the Friar will arrange for Romeo to come and take her away to Mantua. Juliet returns home and apologizes to her father, who moves the wedding forward to Wednesday, the next day. That night, Juliet takes the potion. The next morning, the family find her – apparently dead. The Friar tells them to place her in the tomb.

Act 5

Unfortunately, Romeo does not get the Friar's message. Instead he hears from Balthasar that Juliet is dead. Romeo buys a poison and resolves to die with Juliet in the tomb. He arrives in Verona late that night. The Friar finds out that his message has not been delivered and rushes to the tomb to be there when Juliet wakes up.

Romeo arrives at the tomb and tries to break in. When Paris tries to arrest him, they fight and Paris is killed. Romeo enters the tomb and finds Juliet's body. He takes the poison and dies instantly. The Friar arrives just as Juliet wakes up, and tries to persuade her to leave. She refuses. When he is gone, she stabs herself with Romeo's dagger. The Prince, the Capulets, and Lord Montague arrive to find the three young people dead. The Friar explains what has happened. The Prince blames the feud for the tragedy. Montague and Capulet shake hands.

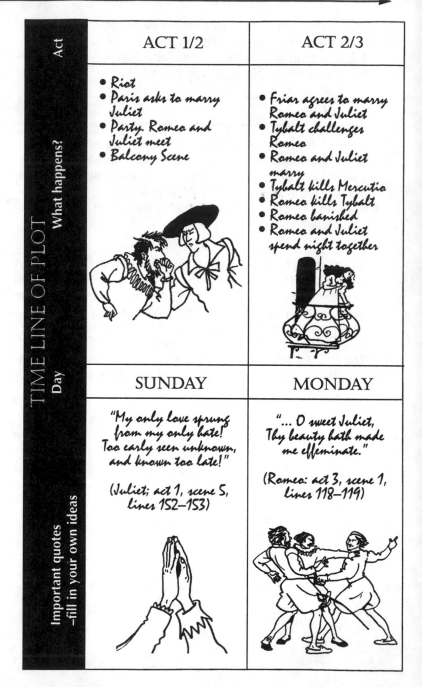

	ACT 1/2	ACT 2/3
Act		
What happens?	• Riot • Paris asks to marry Juliet • Party. Romeo and Juliet meet • Balcony Scene	• Friar agrees to marry Romeo and Juliet • Tybalt challenges Romeo • Romeo and Juliet marry • Tybalt kills Mercutio • Romeo kills Tybalt • Romeo banished • Romeo and Juliet spend night together
Day	SUNDAY	MONDAY
Important quotes –fill in your own ideas	"My only love sprung from my only hate! Too early seen unknown, and known too late!" (Juliet; act 1, scene 5, lines 152–153)	"... O sweet Juliet, Thy beauty hath made me effeminate." (Romeo: act 3, scene 1, lines 118–119)

TIME LINE OF PLOT

6

ACT 3/4	ACT 4	ACT 5
• Romeo leaves • Lord Capulet insists Juliet marry Paris on Thursday • Friar's plan to pretend Juliet dead • Lord Capulet moves wedding forward to Wednesday • Juliet takes potion 	• Juliet found "dead" 	Morning • Romeo hears of Juliet's "death," buys poison and travels to Verona Night • Friar finds out his letter to Romeo was not delivered • Romeo arrives at Capulet tomb • Romeo kills Paris and then himself • Juliet awakens, refuses to go with Friar, and kills herself • Prince, Capulet, and Lord Montague arrive
TUESDAY	WEDNESDAY	THURSDAY
"Hang thee, young baggage, disobedient wretch! I tell thee what, get thee to church a Thursday, Or never after look me in the face." (Lord Capulet: act 3, scene 5, lines 166–168) 	"O son, the night before thy wedding day Hath Death lain with thy wife." (Lord Capulet: act 4, scene 5, lines 41–42) 	"Capulet, Montague? See what a scourge is laid upon your hate, That heaven finds means to kill your joys with love!" (Prince Escalus: act 5, scene 3, lines 301–303)

Who's Who

The Mini Mind Map above asks questions about the character of Romeo. After you have read this chapter, test yourself by looking at the full Mind Map on p. 13, and then copying the Mini Mind Map and trying to add to it from memory.

The families

The Montagues and the Capulets are two wealthy and important families in Verona. Due to an *ancient grudge*, which is never explained, the two families are bitter enemies.

Romeo

Romeo is the son of Lord and Lady Montague. His best friends are Benvolio and Mercutio. He is clever, excelling at the kind of elaborate wordplay that was popular in Elizabethan times. He uses witty puns when he jokes with his friends and elaborate and stylish poetry when he talks about love. At the beginning of the play, Romeo is infatuated with Rosaline and his language is clever but artificial. Later, when he falls in love with Juliet, his language becomes simpler and more sincere.

*Rom*eo's name reflects his *rom*antic nature. He is passionate and a bit of a dreamer. His emotions are the most important thing to him and he hardly notices what is going on in the real world. For example, at the beginning of the play he is so concerned with his own troubles that he does not notice that a riot has occurred. When he meets Juliet, his love for her becomes the most important thing in the world and he is determined to do anything in order for them to be together.

Juliet

Juliet is the only daughter of Lord and Lady Capulet. Although Juliet is not quite 14, her parents are already making plans for her to marry. At the beginning of the play, she is a dutiful daughter who does what her parents tell her. After she meets Romeo she becomes more independent. She defies her parents by secretly marrying Romeo, spending the night with him in her own house, and refusing to marry Paris.

Juliet is a strong character, more practical and down to earth than Romeo. It is she who suggests marriage on the first night they meet and refuses to be impressed by Romeo's clever, artificial love poetry. She insists on Romeo speaking from his heart.

Juliet is always honest with Romeo about her feelings, even if what she says is considered unconventional for a young woman. Juliet is brave and is willing to risk anything in order to be with Romeo; she deceives her parents, lies to her Nurse, swallows a dangerous drug, and eventually kills herself.

Benvolio

Romeo's friend Benvolio is a Montague. He is the first major character we meet and his first words tell us that he is a peacemaker. The name *Benvolio* means "goodwill," reflecting his *benevo*lent character. He is a good friend, a good relative, and a good citizen. Everyone seems to trust Benvolio – Lord and Lady Montague ask him to find out what is troubling their son, Romeo confesses his sorrow to him, and later, the Prince asks him to explain the deaths of Mercutio and Tybalt. Benvolio's calm character provides a balance to the passionate Romeo, the bawdy Mercutio, and the violent Tybalt.

Mercutio

Romeo's friend Mercutio is related to the Prince. The name *Mercu*tio reflects his *mercu*rial nature – quick and volatile. Mercutio can be a good companion. He is lively, noisy, and rude. His language is full of jokes, puns, and sexual double meanings. His view of love is entirely focused on the physical and he mocks Romeo's romantic ideas, sometimes offending his friend. Mercutio's quick temper gets him into trouble when he fights Tybalt on behalf of Romeo and is killed. Mercutio's death is important in sparking the final tragic sequence of events in the play.

Tybalt

Tybalt is Juliet's cousin. His character in the play is one-sided – he is an aggressive, hot-tempered young man who hates all Montagues. At the beginning of the play, he draws Benvolio into a fight. At the Capulet party, he wants to challenge Romeo. Later, when Romeo refuses to fight him, he kills Mercutio.

Lord Capulet

Juliet's father is a wealthy, elderly man who is used to having his own way. He can be an affectionate father and a good host, but, if crossed, his temper is quick and violent. When Juliet is an obedient daughter, he is kind and protective toward her, but when she refuses to obey him, he explodes. He considers Juliet his property to do with as he likes. He also dominates his wife, his relatives, and his servants.

Lady Capulet

Lady Capulet is much younger than her husband and this age gap is referred to several times in the play. Although we do not find out much about the relationship between Lord and Lady Capulet, there is a hint that she is scornful of his age. When he asks for a sword to join in the riot, she suggests a crutch instead. Despite this, she usually gives in to her husband and she agrees with his plans for Juliet to marry Paris.

Lady Capulet's relationship with Juliet is distant and formal. She is cold and unemotional throughout the play except on two occasions: First, when Tybalt dies, she becomes angry and vengeful and demands that Romeo be put to death. Second, when Juliet is thought to be dead, she expresses genuine grief.

The Nurse

The Nurse has looked after Juliet since she was a baby. She cares deeply about Juliet and is willing to help her marry Romeo even though this means going against Lord and Lady Capulet's wishes. In some ways the Nurse is similar to Mercutio. She is lively and talkative and her view of love focuses on the sexual. Just as Mercutio's bawdy humor contrasts with Romeo's romantic view of love, the Nurse's rude jokes highlight the purity of Juliet's love. Juliet relies on the Nurse as her friend and confidante and when the Nurse advises her to marry Paris, Juliet feels betrayed.

Lord Montague

Lord Montague is a caring father to Romeo. At the beginning of the play, he asks Benvolio to find out what is troubling his son. After the fight with Tybalt, he pleads with the Prince not to punish Romeo. At the end of the play, Lord Montague is left alone to grieve over the deaths of his wife and son.

Lady Montague

Lady Montague says very little in the play but, like her husband, she is motivated by concern for Romeo. After Romeo is exiled from Verona, Lady Montague dies of grief.

Friar Lawrence

Friar Lawrence represents the authority of the Church. His advice is respected by everyone in the play and it is to him that Romeo and Juliet go when they have a problem. The Friar advises careful and considered action. He warns that haste is dangerous, but events in the play do not allow time for thought.

When asked to marry Romeo and Juliet, the Friar agrees because he believes it will help to end the feud between the Montagues and the Capulets. By performing this secret marriage, the Friar places himself in a difficult position. When he is later asked to marry Juliet to Paris, he cannot do it. He tries to help Romeo and Juliet, but his plans misfire. At the end, the Friar proves himself a weak man by running away from the tomb.

Prince Escalus

The Prince represents law and power. In Shakespeare's time many people believed in the divine right of kings, that monarchs had their authority passed down to them from God. This gave them absolute power. Prince Escalus does not have to consult with anyone else; his word is law. The name *Escalus* means "scales" and this reflects the idea of justice.

Paris

Paris is a typical wealthy young man in Verona. He wants to marry Juliet and so he approaches her father to ask permission. He accepts the decisions of Lord Capulet, and assumes that Juliet will too. Paris' language is always formal and polite. He has a strong sense of honor and this is why he fights with Romeo when he believes that Romeo is desecrating the Capulet tomb.

Over to you

Mind Mapping can help you to explore characters and remember things about them. The Mind Map of Romeo on the opposite page looks at six areas:

1 **Who** is he: age, family, relationships?
2 **When** does he appear: first time, important scenes?
3 **What** is he like: characteristics, language, development?
4 **How** would an actor play him? Ideas about how Romeo might behave.
5 **Why** does he behave as he does? What motivates him?
6 **Quotes** that reveal something about him.

create your own Mind Maps for characters in the play

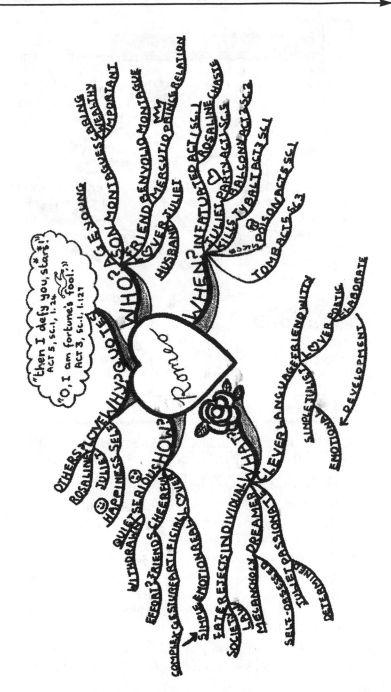

THEMES AND IMAGERY

A **theme** is an idea developed or explored throughout a work. The main themes of *Romeo and Juliet* are shown in the Mini Mind Map above. "Imagery" refers to the kind of word picture used to bring the themes to life. Test yourself on the themes by copying the Mini Mind Map, adding to it yourself, then comparing your results with the full Mind Map on p. 19.

Love

There are many kinds of love in *Romeo and Juliet*. At the center of the play is the love between Romeo and Juliet. This "love at first sight" develops quickly into a strong mutual attachment. The love scenes between Romeo and Juliet are set apart from the haste and bustle of the rest of the play. When the lovers meet, time seems to stand still. Even in the middle of the Capulet party, it is as if Romeo and Juliet are alone together.

Romeo and Juliet are willing to do anything to be with one another, but fate is against them. Their words to each other are tender and intimate but, at the same time, there are many reminders of their tragic destiny.

In contrast to the strength and purity of the love between Romeo and Juliet, the characters of the Nurse, Mercutio,

Sampson, and Gregory revel in their own naughty humor, which is full of double meanings and sexual jokes. They seem to view love only in the physical sense.

Romeo and Juliet marry because their love for each other is so deep. Others in the play see marriage as achieving a particular purpose. Lord and Lady Capulet try to arrange a marriage for Juliet for status and financial gain. Even Friar Lawrence agrees to marry Romeo and Juliet because he thinks it will end the feud. Other expressions of love in the play include the relationships between Romeo, Mercutio, and Benvolio, Romeo and his parents, Juliet and the Nurse, and Juliet and her parents.

Conflict

All drama involves conflict. A story is made interesting by oppositions of people and ideas. In *Romeo and Juliet* there are many forms of conflict. The central one is the feud between the Montagues and the Capulets. There does not seem to be any reason for this *ancient grudge* and yet many people die because of it. Members of each family seem to be governed by a macho code of honor that requires them to hate, insult, and fight each other. Even the household staff becomes caught up in this rivalry. There are other forms of conflict in the play – between men and women, parents and children, the individual and society. As you read the play, you will notice other oppositions. It may help you to Mind Map them.

Two worlds

Another theme in the play is the contrast between the real and the unreal world. People in the real world talk about the body, joking about sexual desire and complaining about aches and pains. They express themselves through gesture and touch, passion and violence. There is an awareness of the physical need for food, sleep, and money. Some of the characters who inhabit this world are Mercutio, with his cynical and physical view of love; the Nurse, with her rude innuendos and awareness of her body's limitations; Tybalt, with his violent nature, and Lord Capulet, with his emphasis on marriage for social and financial gain.

The unreal world is full of poetry and dreams. Romeo inhabits this world most of the time. He lives inside his own head, unaware of the real world going on around him. He idealizes love, placing it out of the physical sphere. He is haunted by dreams, which hint at the real things that will happen to him. Unfortunately for Romeo, the physical world thrusts itself upon him and he is forced to confront the existence of the feud, the violence of Tybalt, and the reality of his banishment.

When Romeo and Juliet are together, they exist in the unreal world. Whenever they are together there is an atmosphere of peace and stillness. They are in a world of love, unaffected by the purely physical concerns of the world around them. This is reinforced by the intrusions of the outside world that interrupt each of their encounters.

Juliet seems to be able to move between the two worlds. Even caught up in romance, she remains aware of what is going on in the real world. It is Juliet who warns Romeo of the danger of being caught in the Capulet garden, suggests marriage, looks forward with eagerness to a night of physical passion, and carries out an intricate plan to escape her marriage to Paris.

Time

The events in Shakespeare's source (Brooke's poem, *The Tragical History of Romeus and Juliet*) take place over several months. Shakespeare condenses this to five days. Romeo and Juliet meet and fall in love on the first day, marry on the second, are parted on the third, and die together on the fifth. There is no time for anyone to consider what to do and decisions are made in a hurry. There is a contrast between the impatience of youth and the caution of old age. The Friar warns Romeo not to be so hasty and Juliet scolds the Nurse for her slowness. Images of lightning and a flower bud are used to describe Romeo and Juliet's love, the bud suggesting a rapid blossoming and the lightning highlighting the brief, fleeting nature of their love. The timing of events is also important.

Romeo's suicide in the tomb only seconds before Juliet awakes is very bad timing. The Friar hurries to the tomb to try to prevent a tragedy, but arrives moments too late.

Fate

Fate is an important theme in the play. The sequence of events that lead up to the deaths of Romeo and Juliet could be seen as coincidence or bad luck. From the Prologue we are told that Romeo and Juliet are *star-crossed* – that fate is against them. Time and again throughout the play, we are reminded that Romeo and Juliet are going to die. It seems as if, whatever they do, the lovers will not be able to avoid this tragic end.

Life and death

The references to life and death throughout the play are linked to the theme of fate. It is Romeo and Juliet's fate to die because of their love and we are often reminded of this. The play is full of images of night, darkness, tombs, graves, poisons, and swords. At the same time, there are many images of light and lightness, suggesting life and love. Romeo talks about Juliet as a *bright angel* shining in the night. Juliet imagines Romeo as *whiter than new snow upon a raven's back*. This contrast between light and dark, life and death, shows how closely the two are linked. Romeo and Juliet are life to each other, but their love for each other brings about their death.

Power

An important theme in *Romeo and Juliet* is power. Some people have the power to tell others what to do. Prince Escalus has absolute authority in Verona. It is his decision who lives and dies. Lord Capulet has complete power over what happens in his household. He expects his wife, his daughter, and his servants to do exactly as he tells them. Friar Lawrence is also in a powerful position. These three men represent the considerable power of the monarchy, patriarchy, and the Church at the time the play was written. But Shakespeare is also aware of the power of individual free will. Characters often ignore the authority of the state, the family, and the Church. The Prince forbids fighting in the street, but Mercutio and Tybalt ignore his orders. Lord Capulet instructs Juliet to marry Paris, but she will not. The Friar lectures on the sin of suicide, but Romeo and Juliet choose this path in order to be united.

Test yourself

? There are 28 words hidden in the box below. All are themes in *Romeo and Juliet*. Words can read forwards and backwards; horizontally, vertically, or diagonally. How many can you find?

S	H	E	Y	P	C	O	N	F	L	I	C	T
R	A	V	E	A	E	H	K	I	A	K	L	E
A	T	O	N	R	G	G	R	J	W	I	C	M
T	E	L	O	E	E	G	A	U	G	N	A	L
S	Y	I	M	N	A	W	D	U	E	F	N	H
R	T	N	T	T	C	B	O	D	G	A	H	O
E	I	J	F	S	E	X	I	P	A	T	T	N
L	R	U	E	M	U	C	R	P	I	U	A	O
I	O	S	I	D	N	L	X	Q	R	A	E	R
G	H	T	L	I	G	H	T	N	R	T	D	U
I	T	I	O	H	T	U	O	Y	A	I	S	T
O	U	C	H	A	N	C	E	F	M	O	M	E
N	A	E	T	G	O	T	H	G	I	N	L	Y

now take a break before beginning the Commentary

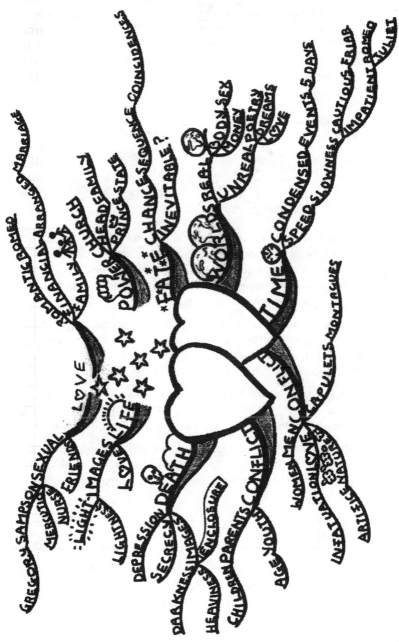

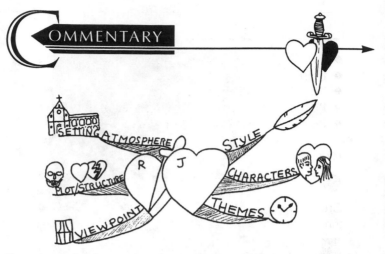

To make reviewing easier, the Commentary looks at each scene in turn, beginning with a brief preview that will prepare you for the scene and help with last-minute reviewing. The Commentary comments on whatever is important in the section, focusing on the areas shown in the Mini Mind Map above.

Wherever there is a focus on a particular theme, the icon for that theme appears in the margin (see p. x for key). Look out, too, for the Style and Language sections. Being able to comment on style and language will help you to get an "A" on your exam.

You will learn more from the Commentary if you use it alongside the play itself. Read a scene from the play, then the corresponding Commentary section – or the other way around.

Remember that when a question appears in the Commentary with a star ✪ in front of it, you should stop and think about it for a moment. And **remember to take a break** after completing each exercise!

Prologue

The **Chorus** introduces the play, summarizing the story that is to come. ✪ From this short description, what would you say are going to be the main themes of the play?

Act 1 *scene* 1

◆ Fight breaks out between Capulets and Montagues.
◆ Benvolio tries to make peace.
◆ Tybalt joins in fight.
◆ Prince declares anyone fighting again will be executed.
◆ Romeo tells Benvolio he is in love.

JOKING

Sampson and Gregory, two of Capulet's servants, boast about their bravery and sexual prowess. Sampson tells Gregory how much he hates the Montagues. ✪ What does he threaten to do to the men and women of the Montague family?

Sampson and Gregory's conversation is full of puns and sexual jokes. Elizabethan audiences were very fond of puns. ✪ How many puns can you find in lines 1–33? Why do you think Shakespeare starts the play like this?

THE RIOT

Sampson and Gregory meet up with two of Montague's servants and a fight breaks out. ✪ What starts the quarrel? Benvolio tries to stop the fight but Tybalt attacks him. Benvolio's first words tell us that he is a peacemaker. ✪ What do Tybalt's words tell us about him? More people join in and soon there is a full-scale riot going on. Lord Capulet and Lord Montague try to join in. ✪ How do Lady Capulet and Lady Montague respond to their husbands' attempts to fight?

THE PRINCE'S DECLARATION

Prince Escalus arrives and calls a halt to the riot. He is furious because there have been three street brawls between the Capulets and Montagues. He threatens to execute anyone disturbing the peace again.

STYLE AND LANGUAGE

Prince Escalus speaks in blank verse. This more formal way of speaking is often used by nobles in Shakespeare's plays. Blank verse, which is unrhymed iambic pentameter, has been one of the most popular verse forms from the fourteenth century to the present day. Each line has ten syllables, divided into five (*pent,* as in pentangle) metrical feet of two syllables each. This length of line is called pentameter. In each metrical foot, the stress is on the second syllable. This kind of rhythm is called iambic. Iambic pentameter can be written as rhyming verse or as unrhymed (blank) verse.

WORRIED ABOUT ROMEO

Lord and Lady Montague talk to Benvolio about Romeo. They are worried about his recent behavior. ❂ What has Romeo been doing that concerns his parents? Benvolio promises to find out what is wrong. Benvolio talks to Romeo alone. Romeo speaks in riddles, but Benvolio discovers that Romeo is in love with a woman who cannot return his love because she has sworn that she will live in chastity. Benvolio advises Romeo to forget her by looking at other women.

STYLE AND LANGUAGE

Romeo's language in this scene is very elaborate, like much Elizabethan love poetry. These are some of the poetic techniques he uses:

- **P**ersonification, talking about Love as if it were a person.
- **I**magery and metaphor, for example, describing love as *a smoke made with the fume of sighs* and *a fire sparkling in lovers' eyes.* Images (word pictures) of light and darkness are used throughout the play.
- **R**hyming couplets – pairs of rhyming lines.
- **O**xymorons (opposites) to reflect his confused state of mind – *O heavy lightness, serious vanity ... Feather of lead, bright smoke, cold fire, sick health.*

You could remember these techniques using the mnemonic PIRO. ❂ Some people think that Romeo's use of these artificial poetic devices means that he is not really in love, just infatuated. What do you think?

Act 1 *scene* 2

- ◆ Paris asks Capulet if he can marry Juliet.
- ◆ Capulet sends a servant to invite people to his party.
- ◆ Benvolio and Romeo meet the servant and find out about the party.

ENDING THE FEUD?

The scene begins in the middle of a conversation between Capulet and Paris. Capulet has been telling Paris about the riot and the Prince's declaration. He says, *'tis not hard, I think/For men so old as we to keep the peace.* ❂ What do you think he means by this? Is he committed to ending the feud?

ASKING FOR JULIET'S HAND

 Paris wants to marry Juliet. Capulet says that she is too young. ❂ How old is Juliet? Capulet says that if Paris can persuade Juliet, he will agree to a marriage. He invites Paris to a party at the Capulet house, and tells him that there he will meet young women other than Juliet. ❂ Why does Capulet mention this?

THE INVITATION

Capulet gives his servant a list of people to invite to the party. The servant cannot read and goes to look for help. He finds Benvolio and Romeo and asks them to help him read the invitation list. We discover that the woman Romeo loves is called Rosaline and that she will be at the party. Even though no Montagues are invited to the party, Benvolio and Romeo decide to gate-crash. ❂ Why does Benvolio want Romeo to go to the party?

 ### STYLE AND LANGUAGE

Look at the servant's lines. They are written in prose instead of verse. Prose is often used for characters lower down the social scale.

Romeo uses a complicated metaphor to insist that his love for Rosaline is true (lines 95–10). He argues that if he saw someone more beautiful than Rosaline, the tears in his eyes would turn into fires and burn his eyes because they would be lying. This speech uses the imagery of light (fire and sun) to talk about love. It is prophetic because Romeo does see someone more beautiful and he is punished. This is an example of "foreshadowing," warning the audience of what is going to happen.

Act 1 *scene* 3

◆ Lady Capulet wants to talk to Juliet but the Nurse keeps interrupting.
◆ Lady Capulet asks Juliet if she would like to marry Paris.

MOTHER AND NURSE

Lady Capulet wants to talk to Juliet alone and sends the Nurse away. Then she changes her mind and asks her to return. ✪ Why do you think she does this? The Nurse rambles on and reminisces about a time when Juliet was a toddler and fell. The Nurse's husband teased Juliet that she would fall backwards (in lovemaking) when she was older. Eventually, both Lady Capulet and Juliet ask the Nurse to be quiet.

MARRIAGE

Whereas the Nurse speaks freely, often using sexual imagery, Lady Capulet seems almost embarrassed to bring up the subject of marriage. It is not until the Nurse introduces the subject that Lady Capulet asks Juliet the question, *How stands your disposition to be married?* She describes Paris to Juliet and asks her daughter if she thinks she could love him. ✪ How do you think Juliet feels about her mother's proposal? If you were an actress playing Juliet, how would you play the lines where she responds to Lady Capulet – *It is an honor that I dream not of ...* (line 71) and – *I'll look to like, if looking liking move ...* (lines 103–105)?

STYLE AND LANGUAGE

The Nurse and Lady Capulet speak and act very differently. The Nurse is loud, coarse, and chatty. She uses slang and

shortened words. The rhythm of her language is uneven –
sometimes in verse, sometimes in prose. She repeats
conversations and tells stories. She interrupts herself and others
and cannot seem to keep quiet. Lady Capulet is much more
formal. She says only what is necessary. Her lines are short,
factual, and to the point. She expects the same kind of response
from her daughter, asking her to *Speak briefly*. The only time
that Lady Capulet speaks at length is when she describes Paris
(lines 85–100), in rhyming verse and using a book metaphor.
This way of speaking could be compared to Romeo's love
poetry about Rosaline – clever but artificial.

Test yourself

Questions (answers on p. 26)
1   Divide the following into Capulets and Montagues:
    Sampson, Balthasar, Gregory, Tybalt, Benvolio, Abraham.
2   What lines in Act 1, scene 1 show us that Benvolio is a
    peacemaker?
3   Which of these characters would be more likely to speak in
    prose, and which in blank verse? Romeo, Nurse, Servant,
    Prince Escalus.
4   When Benvolio finds out that Romeo is in love with
    Rosaline, what does he tell him to do? Find the lines in
    Act 1, scene 1 and Act 1, scene 2, where Benvolio gives
    advice to Romeo.
5   Why is Capulet having a party? Where will it be held? Who
    is invited? Who isn't?

Assignment

?   Fill in the gaps in this extract from the Prologue. Don't
    refer to the text. It doesn't matter if you use different
    words as long as they are appropriate. You can stick to
    the original story, or use this opportunity to vary the
    time, setting, or characters.

    Two households, both alike in _____,
    In fair _____ (where we lay our scene),
    From ancient grudge break to new _____,
    Where _____ blood makes _____ hands
    unclean.

From forth the _____ of these two foes
A pair of _____ takes their life:
Whose misadventured _____
Doth with their _____ bury their parents' strife.

Think about ...

? Look at the conversation between Benvolio and Romeo in Act 1, scene 1. Read the lines aloud (from line 163 – *Good morrow, cousin* – to the end of the scene). Romeo can't seem to keep his mind on one thing for very long. He speaks in broken phrases, half lines, and riddles. He constantly interrupts himself (*Was that my father that went hence so fast?; Where shall we dine? O me! what fray was here?*). Imagine you are directing the play. How should the actor playing Romeo play this scene? What body movements would match Romeo's words? How should Benvolio respond to Romeo?

Answers

1 **Capulets**: Sampson, Gregory, Tybalt.
  Montagues: Abraham, Balthasar, Benvolio.

2 *Part fools! Put up your swords; you know not what you do* (Act 1, scene 1, lines 65–66).
  I do but keep the peace; put up thy sword,/ Or manage it to part these men with me (Act 1, scene 1, lines 69–70).

3 Prose: Nurse, Servant. Blank verse: Romeo, Prince Escalus.

4 Benvolio advises Romeo to forget Rosaline and find another woman:
  Be ruled by me, forget to think of her (Act 1, scene 1, line 233).
  Examine other beauties (Act 1, scene 1, line 236).
  Tut, man, one fire burns out another's burning,
  One pain is lessened by another's anguish (Act 1, scene 2, lines 47–48).
  Compare her face with some that I shall show,
  And I will make thee think thy swan a crow
  (Act 1, scene 2, lines 93–94).

5 Why? It is a regular event – *an old accustomed feast* (Act 1, scene 2, line 20).
  Where? At the Capulet home – *my poor house* (Act 1, scene 2, line 24).

Who is invited? *Signor Martino ... ' (invitation list – Act 1, scene 2, lines 69–77).

Who is not invited? Montagues – *if you be not of the house of Montagues, I pray come and crush a cup of wine* (Act 1, scene 2, lines 86–88).

take a short break before joining the party

Act 1 *scene* 4

◆ Romeo, Benvolio, Mercutio, and friends decide how to gate-crash Capulet party.
◆ Mercutio tries to cheer Romeo up with story of Queen Mab.
◆ Romeo feels a sense of doom about going to party.

GATE-CRASHERS

The friends discuss the best way to get into the Capulet party uninvited. Romeo asks if they should recite a speech but Benvolio says that such wordiness (*prolixity*) is out of fashion. He suggests that they perform a dance instead. Romeo says he is too depressed to dance. Mercutio tries to cheer him up by teasing him.

STYLE AND LANGUAGE

Romeo and Mercutio are good friends. Their conversation reflects this. Look at their conversation between *Nay, gentle Romeo, we must have you dance* (line 13) and *Here are the beetle brows shall blush for me* (line 32). They pick up on each other's words, using puns to turn the meanings around. Romeo uses images of weight and heaviness to describe his state of mind. Mercutio encourages him with images of lightness. ✪ What words and phrases in this speech make you think of heaviness and lightness?

QUEEN MAB

Romeo feels a sense of foreboding about the Capulet party. He says *'tis no wit to go*, blaming this feeling on a dream. Mercutio makes fun of Romeo's belief in dreams and claims *That dreamers often lie*. Mercutio then tells a long story about Queen Mab, who brings dreams to people. First he describes her and her carriage, then he explains what she does to dreamers. Mercutio's story is a fairy tale, but there are some unpleasant images in it, especially toward the end. Queen Mab's wagon driver is a *worm/ Pricked from the lazy finger of a maid*, she *plagues* ladies' lips with blisters, brings nightmares to a soldier, tangles the manes of horses and *presses* on young women in an aggressively sexual manner.

Mercutio is finally interrupted by Romeo, who accuses him of talking about *nothing*. Mercutio agrees; he has been talking about dreams. He has made his point, that Romeo should take no notice of his ominous dream.

FOREBODING

Romeo is not convinced. As the friends go off to the party, he expresses a sense of doom: *my mind misgives ... untimely death* (lines 113–118). This is important because Romeo seems to be foretelling his own fate. This foreshadowing warns us that the story will end in tears.
○ Why do you think Romeo goes to the party if he feels like this?

Act 1 *scene 5*

◆ Servants prepare for Capulet party.
◆ Capulet welcomes guests.
◆ Romeo and Juliet meet.
◆ Tybalt furious at Romeo's presence.
◆ Capulet orders Tybalt to restrain himself.

The bustle of servants preparing for the party helps to relieve the tension at the end of Act 1, scene 4. The servants joke and complain to each other and the stage is very busy. ○ If you were directing the play, how would you stage this scene?

THE PARTY

Lord Capulet welcomes his guests. In his first speech he talks to many different people. Read his lines aloud. ✪ How many people or groups of people does he talk to? Try to spot the points where he switches to a new group or individual.

Romeo, who came to the party to see Rosaline, spots Juliet across the crowded room. Despite everything he has said about his love for Rosaline, he falls hopelessly in love with Juliet at first sight.

TYBALT RECOGNIZES ROMEO

Tybalt hears Romeo's voice and recognizes him as a Montague. He is furious and sends his page to get a sword. Tybalt's anger is curbed by Capulet, who insists that Romeo is allowed to stay. ✪ Why do you think Capulet tolerates Romeo's presence? See how Capulet tries to deal with Tybalt and his guests at the same time (lines 86–91). ✪ How should an actor play these lines?

THE LOVERS MEET

At the beginning of line 104, Romeo seems to be in the middle of a conversation with Juliet. Shakespeare does not seem to show the moment when Romeo and Juliet first meet. Look at Romeo's first words, *If I profane with my unworthiest hand ...* . ✪ Do you think these are his first words to Juliet? Romeo and Juliet speak to each other as if they were completely alone, even though they are in the middle of a party. ✪ Have they found a quiet corner, or are they just unaware of everyone around them? They are interrupted in a kiss by the Nurse, who calls Juliet away.

Juliet's last line to Romeo is *You kiss by th'book*. Some people think this means that Romeo kisses perfectly, like an expert lover. But it could also mean that his kiss is artificial, learned from a book, without real emotion, like his elaborate love poetry about Rosaline. ✪ What do you think the line means?

Why do Romeo and Juliet "kiss" like this at first?

STYLE AND LANGUAGE

Romeo's words when he first sees Juliet are a complete contrast to the chatter and noise of the party. He speaks in poetry, using rhyming couplets. If you read the lines aloud you will notice the "o" and "s" sounds. This has the effect of slowing down and softening the lines. Compared to the soft love poetry in Romeo's speech, Tybalt's language is harsh and clipped, reflecting the aggression that he introduces into the action. Romeo and Juliet's words to each other are tender and intimate. This is a direct contrast to Tybalt's angry lines.

Lines 104–117 are written as a **sonnet**, a popular poetic form in Shakespeare's time. Romeo and Juliet take turns speaking the lines of the sonnet. This shows how in tune they are with each other, much as Romeo and Mercutio's sharing of lines and themes in Act 1, scene 4 reflects their good relationship. The sonnet ends with a rhyming couplet (lines 116–117), which is accompanied by a kiss. ✪ Do you think the sonnet's religious imagery is appropriate for a conversation about love? Why do you think Shakespeare uses this imagery?

SONNETS

A sonnet has 14 lines, broken into three sections: the first eight lines, rhyming ABABCDCD; the next four lines, rhyming EFEF and a rhyming couplet at the end, rhyming GG. Sonnets are written in iambic pentameter (see p. 21).

Romeo	If I profane with my unworthiest hand	A
	This holy shrine, the gentle sin is this,	B
	My lips, two blushing pilgrims, ready stand	A
	To smooth that rough touch with a tender kiss.	B
Juliet	Good pilgrim, you do wrong your hand too much,	C
	Which mannerly devotion shows in this,	D
	For saints have hands that pilgrim's hands do touch,	C
	And palm to palm is holy palmers' kiss.	D
Romeo	Have not saints lips, and holy palmers too?	E
Juliet	Ay, pilgrim, lips that they must use in prayer.	F
Romeo	O then dear saint, let lips do what hands do:	E
	They pray, grant thou, lest faith turn to despair.	F
Juliet	Saints do not move, though grant for prayers' sake.	G
Romeo	Then move not while my prayer's effect I take.	G

TRUTH DAWNS

Romeo asks the Nurse who Juliet is and discovers that she is a Capulet. As Romeo is leaving, Juliet sends the Nurse to find out his identity and discovers that he is a Montague. ❂ How do you think Romeo and Juliet feel at this point? What lines give you an indication of their emotions?

CHORUS

The Chorus ends the act, explaining how Romeo has forgotten Rosaline and now loves Juliet. ❂ Do you think these lines show sympathy for Romeo or are they making fun of him? This is the third sonnet in the play (the first was the Prologue at the beginning of Act 1 and the second was the conversation between Romeo and Juliet earlier in this scene).

Test yourself

Questions (answers opposite)

1 What kinds of dreams does Queen Mab bring to the following people: lawyer, parson, lover, lady, courtier, soldier?

2 What does Tybalt threaten to do when he discovers Romeo is at the Capulet party?

3 What does Juliet say when she finds out Romeo is a Montague?

Assignments

? Draw a graph showing how Romeo's mood changes during Act 1. Label the highs and lows with a line from the play that tells you how he feels at these points.

? Find a word or phrase in the Prologue that makes you think of each of the following themes: conflict, fate, love, death.

? List all the puns you can find in Romeo and Mercutio's conversation in Act 1, scene 4, lines 11–32.

? You have been asked to produce an animated cartoon of Mercutio's Queen Mab speech in Act 1, scene 4. The speech falls into two parts: the description of Queen Mab (lines 58–74), and the story of what she does at night (lines 75–100). Write guidelines for the cartoonist, explaining how Queen Mab should be illustrated. The second part of the speech gives you the action for your cartoon. Make a note of exactly what Queen Mab does during the night. How would you represent this in your cartoon? What is the atmosphere of your cartoon – funny, eerie, frightening? Does the atmosphere change from the beginning to the end? You could plan out a storyboard for your cartoon, showing what happens and when, and including instructions for music and voice-over.

? There are many different views of love expressed in Act 1, those of: Sampson and Gregory, Benvolio, Mercutio, the Nurse, Paris, Lady Capulet, Lord

Capulet, Romeo for Rosaline, Romeo for Juliet, Juliet for Paris, Juliet for Romeo. Find one line or phrase that expresses each of these views.

Think about ...

Romeo has already been in love twice so far in the play – in the space of one day! Who does he really love, and why?

Answers

1 Lawyer *fees*, parson *benefice*, lover *love*, lady *kisses*, courtier *cur'sies*, and later *a suit* – receiving money for representing someone at court, soldier *cutting foreign throats*, etc. (Act 1, scene 4, lines 76–88).
2 *Strike him dead* (Act 1, scene 5, line 67).
3 *My only love sprung from my only hate!* (Act 1, scene 5, line 152).

the balcony scene beckons – after the break

Act 2 *scene* 1 ⚔️

- ◆ After the party Romeo returns to Juliet.
- ◆ Benvolio and Mercutio look for him.

This scene is set outside the Capulet house. Romeo has left the party but finds himself drawn back to Juliet. Benvolio and Mercutio call for Romeo, addressing him as *madman! passion! lover!* ✪ Do you think this is a good description of Romeo? Mercutio makes fun of Romeo's obsession with Rosaline (Mercutio does not know that Romeo is now in love with Juliet). ✪ Where is Romeo while Mercutio and Benvolio talk about him? If he can hear what they are saying, how do you think he feels?

Mercutio's lines in this scene are full of sexual puns. Mercutio seems unable to think of love in any other way.

Act 2 *scene* 2

◆ Romeo sees Juliet at her window.
◆ He listens to her speaking and then speaks to her.
◆ They declare their love for each other.

This is one of the most famous scenes in Shakespeare. It is often called the **balcony scene.** Although Shakespeare does not mention a balcony (the stage direction says that Juliet is "aloft as at a window"), many productions have used one. It is important that Juliet is placed above Romeo in this way. They can see each other but they cannot touch. This positioning affects what the characters say and do in the scene. ✪ How might the scene have been different if Romeo and Juliet had met under the trees?

The scene is different from others in the play so far; it takes place at night in the moonlight, in the Capulet garden. After the commotion of earlier scenes, this creates a completely different mood. The only two characters in the scene are Romeo and Juliet. This gives them the chance to tell each other how they feel. They are direct with each other, frankly confessing their love.

ROMEO ENTERS THE CAPULET GARDEN

Romeo's first line refers to Mercutio – he has obviously heard everything that was said in Act 2, scene 1. ✪ If you were playing Romeo, in what tone of voice would you deliver this line?

Romeo looks up at the light in Juliet's window and she appears. The physical relationship between the two characters (Romeo on the ground, Juliet up at a window) is reflected in the language. Romeo refers to Juliet as something above him (*sun, angel, stars, clouds*). This might reflect his feeling that she is out of reach – literally, because she is high above him, metaphorically, because she is so beautiful, or logically, because she is a Capulet. Romeo also uses images of light to talk about Juliet (*sun, stars, twinkle, bright*). ✪ How many references to light and/or things up above can you find in lines 1–35?

The balcony scene – what danger is each lover in?

JULIET SPEAKS

When Juliet speaks, Romeo remains hidden and listens to her. Believing she is alone, Juliet talks about her problem – she loves Romeo but he is a Montague. His name is the trouble; it means that he is her enemy. She wishes that he could throw away his name so that they could love each other.

ROMEO REVEALS HIS PRESENCE

Up until now, Juliet has been unaware that Romeo is in the garden. As soon as he is sure that Juliet loves him, Romeo reveals his presence, promising to give up his name if she will love him. Juliet is startled, but as soon as she realizes it is Romeo, she becomes anxious. She asks him how he got in and why he is there. She reminds him that he could be killed for being there. Juliet's practical concern is a complete contrast to Romeo's idealistic poetry.

Romeo shrugs off her worries, saying that he would rather be killed than live without her love, *My life were better ended by their hate/ Than death prorogued, wanting of thy love* (prorogued = postponed). This is another prophetic, foreshadowing line.

JULIET'S HONESTY

Juliet is embarrassed that Romeo has heard her declare her love for him. She says that if it were not so dark he would see her blushing. She is aware that it would be more conventional for her to have been more distant (*strange*). She is worried that Romeo will think her too easy a conquest, yet she does not deny what she has said. She admits her *true-love passion* and asks him if he loves her. This honesty and directness make Juliet seem very modern. ✪ How might you have expected a young girl in Shakespeare's time to act?

So far in the play Romeo has proved himself to be very clever with language. His riddles, puns, and elaborate love poetry are examples of intelligence and wit. ✪ It is often said that when Romeo meets Juliet, his language becomes simpler and more genuine and that this means he is really in love. Do you agree?

SWEARING THEIR LOVE

Romeo swears his love for Juliet by the moon. She tells him not to swear by the moon, which changes throughout the month, in case his love proves as changeable. He asks what he should swear by. It seems that Romeo is so used to elaborate love poetry that he cannot just say "I love you," but must look for more stylish ways of declaring his feelings.

Juliet becomes impatient with him and tells him not to swear at all. She expresses a fear that their love is *too rash, too unadvised, too sudden,* and compares it to lightning and to a ripening bud. ✪ How do these images relate to the themes of speed and time in the play? Romeo asks Juliet to give him her *faithful vow.* She says that she has already given it, but would freely give it again.

Juliet is called by the Nurse and goes inside, but she cannot tear herself away and soon returns. ✪ How many times does Juliet go inside and come back to Romeo before the end of the scene?

MARRIAGE

It is practical Juliet who mentions marriage and suggests arrangements for contacting each other the next day. She asks Romeo to organize a wedding if he is serious about her and, if he is not, to leave her alone. She does not give Romeo a chance to reply to her request. ✪ Why do you think Juliet wants Romeo to agree to a marriage so quickly? How do you think Romeo feels about the proposal?

Test yourself

Questions (answers on p. 38)
1 How do we know that it is dark in Act 2, scene 2?
2 What will happen to Romeo if anyone finds him in the Capulet garden?
3 What does Juliet ask Romeo to do if his love for her is honorable?

Assignments

? Compare Mercutio's words in Act 2, scene 1, lines 26–32 with Romeo's words in Act 2, scene 2, lines 1–10. Read Mercutio's lines aloud, then Romeo's. What is each character talking about? What is similar about the theme of each speech? What is different about the language used? Make notes on how you think actors should deliver the lines. Include advice on tone, volume, facial expression, and body language.

? Find the following famous lines from Act 2, scene 2. Read each line in context, reading a few lines before it and a few lines after it. What does it mean in the play?

That which we call a rose/ By any other word would smell as sweet.
Parting is such sweet sorrow.
O Romeo, Romeo, wherefore art thou Romeo?

? Look at the speech in which Juliet discovers that she has been overheard by Romeo (Act 2, scene 2, lines 90–111). Rewrite it as if it were being spoken by a young girl in the present day.

Think about ...
If you were staging a production of the play, how would you choreograph Act 2, scenes 1 and 2? Remember that in scene 1 Romeo hides from Mercutio and Benvolio, although he can still hear them. In scene 2, Romeo is hidden at the beginning of the scene, but can see and hear Juliet. Where will you place Juliet? Consider how you will handle the part where Romeo reveals his presence to Juliet – does he step out of the

shadows, jump out of a tree, or something else? How does Juliet respond? How could you suggest the closeness that develops between the lovers during the scene?

Answers

1 Romeo talks of the light from Juliet's window (line 2), which would only be visible in contrast to the darkness around. He contrasts the brightness of Juliet to the night around her (line 30). Juliet asks Romeo, *What man art thou that thus bescreened in night/ So stumblest on my counsel? (lines 56–57).*

2 He will be killed (Act 2, scene 2, line 75).

3 She asks him to send her a message saying where and when he will marry her (Act 2, scene 2, lines 151–153).

now take a break before the wedding

Act 2 *scene* 3

◆ Friar Lawrence gathers herbs.
◆ Romeo tells him about Juliet.
◆ Friar agrees to help.

LIFE AND DEATH

We first meet Friar Lawrence gathering plants and herbs. The speech is full of contrasts (*morn/night, clouds/light, womb/tomb, virtue/vice*). Many of these opposites have to do with life and death. The Friar talks about how plants are able to do good or evil depending on how they are used. One is a poison if eaten but a tonic if smelled. This points forward to the Friar's use of a potion to put Juliet to sleep and Romeo's use of a poison to kill himself, and is another example of foreshadowing.

ROMEO'S CONVERSATION WITH THE FRIAR

Romeo greets the Friar, who asks him why he is up so early. Romeo's reply is full of riddles. The Friar demands that Romeo speak plainly. Romeo explains that he is in love with Juliet, that she loves him, and that they want to get married. The Friar is shocked that Romeo's feelings for Rosaline are so soon forgotten. Nevertheless, he agrees to help Romeo and Juliet, believing that this might end the feud between the Montagues and the Capulets. Romeo tries to hurry the Friar along but the Friar warns, *Wisely and slow, they stumble that run fast.*

Act 2 *scene* 4

◆ Benvolio and Mercutio are still looking for Romeo.
◆ Tybalt has challenged Romeo to a duel.
◆ Romeo arrives and jokes with Mercutio.
◆ The Nurse comes to find out if Romeo has a message for Juliet.

A CHALLENGE

Benvolio and Mercutio wonder where Romeo is – he did not come home from the party last night. They still believe that Romeo is in love with Rosaline. Benvolio tells Mercutio that Tybalt has sent a letter to Romeo's house. Mercutio guesses that it is a challenge to a duel. They talk about how Romeo will respond. Benvolio says that he will *answer it*, meaning that he will agree to fight. Mercutio comments that Romeo is *already dead*, killed by love. Although this is supposed to be a joke, we know that it will turn out to be true. This is another example of foreshadowing.

Mercutio makes fun of Tybalt's fencing style, mocking his delicacy and precision. He also jokes about the language used to describe this type of fighting. ❷ What kind of movements do you think would go with Mercutio's words in lines 20–37?

ROMEO AND MERCUTIO HAVE A PUNNING MATCH

Romeo comes in and Mercutio, as usual, begins to tease him. Romeo is in a much better mood now and gives as good as he gets. The two young men match pun for pun until they are interrupted by the arrival of the Nurse. You will probably need to read lines 39–95 carefully if you want to understand all the puns. It will be no surprise to find out that many of Mercutio's puns are sexual.

ENTER THE NURSE

The Nurse arrives, looking for Romeo. Mercutio mocks her mercilessly and even Romeo and Benvolio cannot resist poking fun at her. ❂ Do you think this part of the scene (lines 104–146) is funny or do you feel sorry for the Nurse?

After Benvolio and Mercutio leave, the Nurse complains about the way she has been treated and shouts at her servant Peter for not protecting her. She then turns to the reason why she is there – to find out Romeo's intentions toward Juliet. She expresses concern for Juliet and warns Romeo to treat her fairly. Romeo, after a few interruptions, eventually manages to explain to the Nurse that he has arranged for a marriage this afternoon. The Nurse is delighted and chatters away.

Unknown to her, however, her words contain warnings of the future. She talks about Juliet being pale (as in death) and she links Romeo with rosemary (the flower of remembrance).

This scene is written in prose, which reflects the casual style of conversation. The only time that verse is used is when Romeo talks about Juliet (lines 183–186 and 190–196). ❂ This has the effect of making these lines seem more important. Why would Shakespeare want to do this?

Act 2 scene 5

◆ Juliet is impatient for the Nurse's return.
◆ The Nurse arrives, but avoids giving Juliet the message.
◆ Eventually, she tells Juliet that Romeo has arranged a marriage.

IMPATIENCE

Juliet sent the Nurse to meet Romeo at nine o'clock. According to Act 2, scene 4, the Nurse did not meet Romeo until midday. Juliet has reason to be impatient. Why do you think the Nurse is so late? Juliet's speech links swiftness with youth and slowness with old age. When the Nurse arrives, Juliet wants to hear her news, but the Nurse delays, complaining about her aches and pains.

✪ How many times does the Nurse refer to her bodily discomforts between lines 26 and 69?

Juliet becomes more and more impatient. She mentions the words *tell, speak, say,* or *says* in almost every line, showing how desperate she is for the Nurse to give her Romeo's message. The Nurse refuses to get to the point, grumbling and asking irrelevant questions (*have you dined at home?* and *where is your mother?*). ✪ Why do you think she keeps Juliet waiting like this?

Eventually, the Nurse tells Juliet the news: Romeo will marry her today, in Friar Lawrence's cell. The Nurse sends Juliet off to church, joking that although she is working hard for Juliet now, it will be Juliet who will soon have to *bear the burden* (in lovemaking).

Act 2 *scene* 6

◆ Romeo and Juliet meet in Friar Lawrence's cell to get married.

FATE

Romeo and Juliet are about to get married. It should be a joyful occasion, but many of the lines remind us of the lovers' tragic destiny. Friar Lawrence hopes that sorrow will not follow Romeo and Juliet's wedding. Romeo defies *love-devouring Death* to do what it can to spoil his happiness. The Friar warns that *violent delights have violent ends.* Throughout the play, Romeo stands up to fate. At the end of Act 1, scene 5, he ignores the warnings of his dream. Here, he deliberately challenges Death. In Act 5, scene 1, when he hears of Juliet's "death" after she takes poison, he declares: *then I defy you, stars!* Fate is very important in Shakespeare's plays and, even today, some people might say that Romeo is "tempting fate." ✪ Do you think Romeo is unwise to stand up to fate in this way?

 ### STYLE AND LANGUAGE

When Juliet arrives, Romeo welcomes her with the kind of elaborate poetry we expect from him, playing on the two meanings of the word "measure" (1. quantity and 2. meter of rhyme or music). He asks her to declare her love for him. Juliet replies that *words* and *ornament* (referring to the artifice of poetry) cannot express true love. Yet again, Juliet seems to be insisting that simple, direct expressions of feeling are better than clever but contrived poetry. It is worth remembering, however, that even Juliet's "simple" language is still poetry, written by Shakespeare using formal rhythm and rhyme structures and other poetic devices. ❂ What is the difference between Romeo's language and Juliet's language?

Test yourself

Questions (answers below)
1   What time of day is it in these scenes: (a) Act 2, scene 3; (b) Act 2, scene 4; (c) Act 2, scene 5?
2   Find the lines that tell you that Tybalt has challenged Romeo to a duel.
3   What message does Romeo ask the Nurse to give Juliet?
4   Find the lines that tell you how Romeo intends to reach Juliet's bedroom the night after they are married.

Assignments
?   Look at the Friar's speech in Act 2, scene 3, lines 1–37. Make lists of all the words and phrases that have to do with (a) life and (b) death.
?   In Act 2, scene 4, Romeo describes Mercutio as *a gentleman ... that loves to hear himself talk*. Is this is a fair description? Do you like Mercutio? Make a Mind Map of his good and bad points.

Think about ...
What does Friar Lawrence think of Romeo's feelings for Juliet? Why does he agree to help them marry?

Answers
1   (a) Just before dawn: *The grey-eyed morn smiles on the frowning night* (line 1); *... ere the sun advance his burning eye* (line 5).

(b) Midday: ... *the prick of noon* (line 115).

(c) Midday: *Now is the sun upon the highmost hill* (lines 9–10).

2 **Benvolio:** *Tybalt, the kinsman to old Capulet,/ Hath sent a letter to his father's house.* **Mercutio:** *A challenge, on my life.* (Act 2, scene 4, lines 7–9).

3 Romeo tells the Nurse to ask Juliet to make an excuse to go to confession at Friar Lawrence's cell (room) this afternoon. He will meet her there and they will be married (Act 2, scene 4, lines 183–186).

4 ... *cords made like a tackled stair,/ Which to the high top-gallant of my joy/ Must be my convoy in the secret night* (Act 2, scene 4, lines 192–194);
I must another way,/ To fetch a ladder, by the which your love/ Must climb a bird's nest soon when it is dark. (Act 2, scene 5, lines 77–79).

take a break and prepare for some bloodshed

Act 3 *scene* 1

- ◆ Benvolio and Mercutio meet Tybalt on the streets of Verona.
- ◆ Romeo arrives. Tybalt tries to make him fight.
- ◆ Romeo refuses. Mercutio fights instead and is killed by Tybalt.
- ◆ Romeo fights Tybalt and kills him.
- ◆ The Prince banishes Romeo from Verona.

ON THE STREETS

All the scenes involving Benvolio, Mercutio, and Romeo take place on the streets of Verona. Whereas Juliet's appearances are confined to her father's house, Friar Lawrence's cell, and the tomb, the young men in the play are seen out in the world. Sometimes they are going somewhere, but often they are just "hanging out," chatting to each other and to whoever else comes along. Occasionally, this leads to trouble, as in Act 1, scene 1, when a servants' quarrel leads to a riot involving Benvolio and Tybalt. In this scene, Benvolio seems to be aware that roaming the streets on such a hot day might lead to trouble. He tries to persuade Mercutio to *retire.*

BENVOLIO THE QUARRELER?

Mercutio teases Benvolio with accounts of his quarrelsome nature. ❂ Do you think that Mercutio's description of Benvolio in lines 5–31 is accurate? Benvolio replies that if he were as quarrelsome as Mercutio he would be dead within an hour and a quarter. This foreshadows the tragic events that will follow later in the scene.

TYBALT SEEKS ROMEO

Tybalt arrives, looking for Romeo. Mercutio insults him and tries to provoke a fight. Benvolio warns them that people are watching. He seems to remember the Prince's warning that anyone caught fighting in public again will be sentenced to death. Tybalt, however, is not interested in fighting with Mercutio. As soon as Romeo arrives, Tybalt insults Romeo and challenges him to fight, but Romeo is now married to Juliet. Tybalt is his cousin by marriage. He does not want to get into a fight with him and refuses to become upset by Tybalt's insults. Mercutio is horrified by Romeo's response and calls it *calm, dishonorable, vile submission.* ❂ What do you think Tybalt and Benvolio think of Romeo's behavior?

STYLE AND LANGUAGE

Romeo reflects Tybalt's words back at him. Whereas Tybalt's words are intended to pick a quarrel, Romeo uses them to try to avoid one. Look at the words "love" (lines 61 and 63), "villain" (lines 62 and 65), "injuries" (line 67), and "injured" (line 69) to see how this works.

MERCUTIO FIGHTS AND IS HURT

Mercutio obviously sees Romeo's refusal to fight Tybalt as a cowardly act. Still as keen to fight as he was earlier in the scene, he draws his sword on Tybalt, who now returns his challenge. Romeo tries to make them stop, calling on Benvolio to help him. Benvolio is usually a peacemaker. ❂ Why do you think he is silent when Romeo asks him to intervene between Mercutio and Tybalt? Eventually, Romeo steps between Mercutio and Tybalt, hoping this will stop them, but Tybalt thrusts his sword under Romeo's arm, wounding Mercutio.

Who is hurt, and how did it happen?

MERCUTIO'S DEATH

At first, Benvolio and Romeo are not aware of the seriousness of Mercutio's injury. Mercutio continues joking, seemingly more worried about the fact that Tybalt has escaped without damage. He laughs off his own injury, calling it *a scratch*. Despite this brave face, Mercutio does seem to be aware that the wound is fatal, saying, *I am sped; marry, 'tis enough; I am peppered ... for this world*. He even manages to turn the tragic situation into a pun, *Ask for me tomorrow, and you shall find me a grave man*. ✪ When do you think Benvolio and Romeo realize that Mercutio is going to die? Mercutio dies offstage and Benvolio brings Romeo the news.

REVENGE

Romeo feels guilty about Mercutio's death. He believes that Mercutio only stepped in to fight Tybalt because he refused. Romeo blames Juliet for making him cowardly, *O sweet Juliet,/ Thy beauty hath made me effeminate.* When Tybalt reappears, Romeo fights him and kills him. Benvolio tells Romeo to run away, warning that the Prince will sentence him to death if he is found.

WHOSE FAULT?

When Mercutio is dying he twice curses, *A plague a'both your houses!* He seems to blame the feud between the Capulets and Montagues for his injury. He also blames Romeo. *Why the dev'l came you between us? I was hurt under your arm.* Romeo blames himself for allowing Mercutio to fight Tybalt on his behalf. He implies that it is Juliet's fault for softening his courage. He also blames fate, calling himself *fortune's fool.* On the other hand, Mercutio had been trying to provoke a fight with Tybalt earlier in the scene. And surely it should be Tybalt who takes the blame for Mercutio's death? ❂ Why was Mercutio killed in this scene? Is it possible to blame his death on any of the characters? Some people say that Shakespeare needed to kill the strong character of Mercutio at this stage in order to focus on the two lovers. What do you think?

THE PRINCE'S JUDGMENT

Prince Escalus arrives and asks Benvolio to explain what has happened. As in Act 1, scene 1, Benvolio is called upon to provide a faithful account of events. Benvolio retells the events of the scene. Lady Capulet argues that Benvolio is biased because he is related to the Montagues. ❂ Do you think he gives an accurate account?

Lady Capulet demands that Romeo be put to death for killing Tybalt. Lord Montague argues that Romeo was only doing what the law would have done – killing Tybalt because he had killed Mercutio. ❂ Can you think of any reason for Lord Capulet and Lady Montague remaining silent in this scene? The Prince decides to pass a lighter sentence than earlier threatened. He allows Romeo to live, but exiles him from Verona. If Romeo is found in the city he will be executed.

STYLE AND LANGUAGE

Lady Capulet's interruption (lines 154–158) is interesting. For the first time, her language is uncontrolled. The short sentences, the exclamation marks, the repetition of "o" sounds, seem to indicate a real emotional reaction. Many people criticize Lady Capulet's character for being cold and unfeeling, but here, and in Act 4, scene 5, when she thinks Juliet is dead, her reaction seems to be one of genuine grief. Her words emphasize the importance of family: *cousin, brother's child, husband, kinsman, blood of ours.* However, by her next speech (line 185), she recovers herself sufficiently to demand vengeance. Her language is controlled again as she asks for the death of a Montague in order to compensate for the death of a Capulet. She can see only punishment in terms of the feud.

Act 3 *scene* 2

◆ Juliet impatiently awaits the arrival of Romeo.
◆ The Nurse arrives with the news that Romeo has killed Tybalt and has been banished.
◆ Juliet experiences strong emotional reactions.

JULIET'S WEDDING SONG

This speech is similar to the one at the beginning of Act 2, scene 5, where Juliet is impatient for the Nurse's arrival, but Juliet is no longer the girl she was then. Now she is a married woman longing for her wedding night. The imagery she uses reflects her sexual desire as well as picking up on other themes in the play.

Juliet begins with talk of speed. Here and in Act 2, scene 5, she wants to hurry events along even though earlier (Act 2, scene 2, lines 124–127) she expressed concern that things were moving too swiftly. Juliet talks of the sun (*Phoebus*) going home and night spreading its *close curtain.* Juliet has no doubt about what night means for her and Romeo. She personifies *love-performing Night,* aware that the darkness will mean that Romeo can come secretly to her bedroom. Juliet's language is frankly sexual. She imagines what will happen when Romeo arrives, how she will be nervous and embarrassed at first, later growing bold.

She contrasts the darkness of night with the brightness of Romeo who is *day in night*, imagining his pale body against the darkness like *new snow upon a raven's back*. This is similar to the imagery Romeo uses in Act 2, scene 2, when he talks of Juliet shining in the darkness like the sun and the stars.

This light and dark imagery also has a more ominous overtone, looking forward to the darkness of the tomb and death. Juliet refers to when she will "die." For an Elizabethan audience, to die meant to have an orgasm. Juliet may have this pleasurable image in mind, but she also foretells her own fate.

THE NURSE BRINGS NEWS

When the Nurse enters, her language is confused and emotional. Whereas in Act 2, scene 5, she held back news to tease Juliet, now she seems genuinely unable to deliver the news in a clear and comprehensible way. This leads to a misunderstanding: Juliet thinks that Romeo is dead.

Despite the tragic situation, Shakespeare introduces a pun, shared by Juliet and the Nurse in lines 49–57, on the sounds "ay," "I," and "eye." This only adds to the confusion. Eventually, the Nurse makes the situation plain: *Tybalt is gone and Romeo banished/ Romeo that killed him, he is banished*.

JULIET'S REACTION

Once Juliet realizes what has happened, her first reaction is horror that the person she loved so much has shown himself to be a murderer. Her speech uses oxymorons (opposites), which show her conflicting emotions toward Romeo. He has a *serpent heart* but a *flow'ring face*. He is a *fiend angelical* and *a damned saint*. At this moment Juliet seems to hate Romeo, but when the Nurse agrees and wishes shame on Romeo, Juliet turns on her furiously, *Blistered be thy tongue/ For such a wish!* ❂ Why do you think Juliet reacts like this?

Juliet's mood now changes. She apologizes to Romeo for doubting him and tries to justify his actions to herself. She argues that he must have killed Tybalt because Tybalt would have killed him. She is grateful that Romeo is still alive. Then Juliet remembers that Romeo has been banished and says that this is as bad as if her father, mother, Tybalt, Romeo, and she were dead. She looks at the rope ladder, by which Romeo was to have climbed into her bedroom, and tells the Nurse that it is useless now. The Nurse feels sorry for her and promises to get Romeo to come to her tonight as originally planned.

Act 3 *scene* 3

◆ The Friar tells Romeo that he is banished.
◆ Romeo complains that banishment is worse than death. The Friar tries to reason with him.
◆ The Nurse asks Romeo to visit Juliet.
◆ The Friar thinks of a plan to reunite Romeo and Juliet.

BANISHMENT

The Friar tells Romeo that the Prince has passed *a gentler judgement* than death – banishment. Romeo immediately responds that death would be better than banishment. Why does he say this? The Friar tells Romeo he is being ungrateful and reminds him that under the law the Prince could have had him executed. Romeo replies that it is torture to be away from Juliet, where every living creature can look at her but he cannot. Romeo foreshadows the ending of the play when he asks the Friar if he will give him a *poison* or a *sharp-ground knife* to kill himself instead of being banished. At the end, Romeo kills himself with poison; Juliet kills herself with a knife.

Every time the Friar tries to reason with Romeo, he refuses to listen. The Friar becomes quite impatient and Romeo accuses him of not being able to understand because he is too old.
✪ Read up to line 77. Do you feel sorry for Romeo or do you think he is overreacting?

THE NURSE ARRIVES

Someone knocks at the door and the Friar tries to get Romeo to hide. ✪ Look at lines 78–79. Which lines does the Friar address to Romeo and which to the person at the door? What do you think Romeo is doing during this time? The Nurse enters and sees Romeo weeping on the floor. She says that Juliet is in exactly the same situation. ❂ Would you agree that, in the previous scene, Juliet was behaving like this?

The Nurse urges Romeo to *stand* and *be a man* for Juliet's sake. The sexual overtones are clear – she wants Romeo to come and spend his wedding night with Juliet. At this point, Romeo seems to revive and asks the Nurse for news of Juliet. He wants to know if she hates him because he has murdered her cousin. He curses his name, as if it is this that has caused all the trouble. This reminds us of Juliet's speech in Act 2, scene 2, lines 46–52, where she questions *What's in a name?* Romeo works himself into a frenzy and threatens to cut his name out of his body with a dagger.

THE FRIAR'S SPEECH

Friar Lawrence finally loses patience with Romeo and the Friar's long speech (lines 118–168) seems intended to put Romeo in his place. It can be divided into three sections. (Keywords are in **bold type** to help you remember.)

1 (lines 118–144) The Friar **rebukes** Romeo for trying to commit suicide. He accuses him of being as emotional as a woman and as wild as a beast. He argues that Romeo has already killed Tybalt. By killing himself Romeo will also kill Juliet, who lives for him. The Friar says that Romeo puts his looks (*shape*), love, and intelligence (*wit*) to shame with this behavior.

2 (lines 145–155) The Friar **reminds** Romeo of the reasons he has for being happy: Juliet is alive, Tybalt would have killed him if he had not killed Tybalt, the Prince has turned the sentence of death into one of exile. The Friar scolds Romeo for being so ungrateful.

3 (lines 156–168) The Friar thinks of a **plan** by which Romeo and Juliet can be together. Romeo is to go to Juliet, but leave before dawn, then live in Mantua until a suitable time, when the Friar will tell everyone of the marriage, ask the Prince's forgiveness, and reconcile everyone. The Friar sends the Nurse off to urge the Capulet household to retire early so that Romeo can secretly enter Juliet's bedroom.

Test yourself

Questions (answers on p. 52)

1   Who kills whom in Act 3, scene 1?
2   Fill in the blanks in the following list of oxymorons used
    by Juliet when she finds out Romeo has killed Tybalt (Act
    3, scene 2, lines 79–91).
    serpent _____/_____ face
    _____ tyrant/fiend _____
    _____ raven/_____ lamb
    _____ saint/honorable _____
3   What plan does Friar Lawrence think of to reunite Romeo
    and Juliet after Romeo is banished?

Assignments

?   How many moods does Juliet go through in Act 3, scene
    2? Find one word or phrase that expresses each emotion.
?   When Benvolio explains the events of Act 3, scene 1,
    lines 160–184, he tells the Prince about the actions of
    four people (Tybalt, Romeo, Mercutio, and himself).
    Read the speech to yourself, marking the places where
    Benvolio refers to an action. Then read it again, aloud,
    and act out the parts of each character as Benvolio
    describes them. Take your clues from the words, such
    as *knees humbly bowed, with one hand beats, cries
    aloud,* and so on. You will find an action to represent
    in nearly every line. Be as over the top as you like; it
    doesn't matter if the effect is humorous; it will help
    you to fix it in your memory.

Think about ...

It is difficult to imagine the fight scenes in *Romeo and Juliet*
just by reading the words on the page. Look at the two fights
in Act 3, scene 1, and decide how you would stage them.
How long would each take? Would the characters say their
lines while fighting? How would they communicate through
facial expression and body language? How much would they
move around? What would the other characters in the scene
be doing? How would your choices affect the meaning of the
scene?

Answers

1 Tybalt kills Mercutio; Romeo kills Tybalt.
2 serpent heart/ flow'ring face
   Beautiful tyrant/ fiend angelical
   Dove-feathered raven/ wolvish-ravening lamb
   damned saint/ honorable villain
3 Romeo spends his wedding night with Juliet, but leaves
   before dawn. Romeo lives in Mantua until a suitable time,
   when the Friar will tell everyone of the marriage, ask the
   Prince's forgiveness, and reconcile everyone.

it's time for the lovers to part and for you to take a break

Act 3 *scene* 4

◆ Capulet promises he will persuade Juliet to marry Paris.
◆ He arranges the wedding for Thursday – three days away.

CHANGE OF HEART

Lord Capulet explains to Paris that he has not been able
to ask Juliet if she wants to marry him because of Tybalt's
death. Lady Capulet agrees. Juliet is too upset tonight but she
will ask her in the morning. Then Lord Capulet changes his
mind. He tells Paris that he is certain that Juliet will do what
he tells her and arranges the wedding for Thursday. He asks
Lady Capulet to go to Juliet and tell her the news.

CAPULET'S FEELINGS FOR TYBALT

Look at the first four lines of this scene. This is the first time
Capulet has spoken since Tybalt' s death. He seems to see the
death as an inconvenience that has delayed the marriage of
Paris and Juliet. His cold *Well, we were born to die* contrasts
strongly with Lady Capulet's emotional reaction in Act 3,
scene 1, and Juliet's grief in Act 3, scene 2. When arranging
the wedding, he realizes that people might think it strange if
the family celebrated so soon after Tybalt's death, so he tells
Paris that there will be no great festivities. Keep an eye on the
preparations for the wedding in Act 4, scenes 2 and 4, to see if
Capulet keeps his word.

Act 3 *scene* 5

◆ Dawn arrives and Romeo and Juliet part.
◆ Lady Capulet comes to tell Juliet about the wedding to Paris.
◆ Juliet refuses to marry Paris and Lord Capulet loses his temper with her.
◆ The Nurse urges Juliet to marry Paris. Juliet rejects her as a friend.

DAWN

Romeo and Juliet disagree about whether it is dawn or not. Romeo says he heard a lark and can see light in the sky. Juliet wants Romeo to stay with her. She insists it was a nightingale (a bird that sings at night) and that the light he can see is a meteor. Romeo says that he will stay if Juliet wants him to, even if he is taken and put to death. Juliet finally agrees that dawn is coming and tells him to go. Their conversation reflects the light and dark theme in the play.

Throughout the play, they have only been together during the hours of darkness (except for the few brief moments in Friar Lawrence's cell before their wedding). Now that light is coming, they must be parted again. They will only be reunited in the darkness of the tomb and death. Throughout their conversation, we are aware that Lady Capulet is on her way to Juliet's bedroom (Lord Capulet asked her to go and see Juliet at the end of the last scene). ❂ How does this knowledge affect our enjoyment of the scene?

LADY CAPULET ARRIVES

The Nurse enters and warns Romeo and Juliet that Lady Capulet is coming. The joking between the lovers ends and they say good-bye. In their last words to each other they speak of death. Ominous references, which have appeared throughout the play, occur more often now as events seem to snowball toward the tragedy at the end of the play.

Lady Capulet enters and speaks to Juliet. She thinks Juliet is still weeping over Tybalt's death and scolds her for taking too long over her grief. Lady Capulet's feelings are concentrated on vengeance. The Prince denied her demand (in Act 3, scene 1) that Romeo be executed. Now she vows to Juliet that she will arrange for someone to kill Romeo.

Juliet's reply to her mother is full of double meaning. Look at lines 98–107. ✪ How could you read these lines in different ways to bring out the different meanings?

LADY CAPULET'S NEWS

Lady Capulet tells Juliet that she has some news that will cheer her up. Juliet is very polite to her mother until she finds out what this news is. When she discovers that her parents expect her to marry Paris, the dutiful daughter rebels. Juliet flatly refuses. Compare her politeness in lines 110–111 and 116 with her ourburst in lines 121–128. ✪ How would an actress playing Juliet deliver these lines?

LORD CAPULET ARRIVES

Lord Capulet's lines in this scene can be divided into five sections. (Keywords are in **bold type** to help you remember.)

1 (lines 131–143) Capulet enters already talking. His tone is light and he shows **fatherly concern** for Juliet's tears, which he assumes are for Tybalt. The image of a storm that he conjures up is ironic for, any minute now, a storm is about to erupt between Capulet and Juliet. He asks Lady Capulet if she has told Juliet about the wedding arrangements. Look at Lady Capulet's reply (lines 144–145). ✪ Do you think she means what she says?

2 (lines 146–150) Capulet does not seem to understand at first. As he realizes that Juliet is rejecting Paris, he **accuses** her of being ungrateful. ✪ Why does he refer to Juliet as "she" in this section? Juliet tries to answer his questions without offending him. She says she is grateful for what he has done. She realizes that he means well, but she cannot be proud of what she hates. ✪ Who or what does she hate – Paris, the idea of an arranged marriage, or something else?

Who is angry, and why?

3   (lines 154–162) Juliet's answer enrages Capulet even more.
    He **explodes** at her riddles and puts his foot down. He
    orders her to go to the church with Paris on Thursday;
    otherwise he will drag her there. Look at the harsh words
    he uses to describe Juliet (lines 161–162). If you were an
    actor playing Capulet, what actions would you use to
    accompany these words? Lady Capulet interrupts at this
    point, saying: *Fie, fie, what, are you mad?* ✪ What has
    happened to make her say this? Is her comment directed at
    Lord Capulet or Juliet? Juliet falls on her knees before her
    father and pleads with him.

4   (lines 166–175) Capulet **repeats** his order that Juliet must
    go to church on Thursday or never look at him again. His
    line: *Speak not, reply not, do not answer me!/ My fingers
    itch* hints at the violent anger he is just managing to
    contain. He cannot even allow himself to listen to Juliet or
    talk to her. He cuts her off completely for a few moments.
    At this point the Nurse interrupts to defend Juliet. Capulet
    tries to silence her with cruel and sarcastic comments. The
    Nurse persists for a while and finally gives up. Even Lady
    Capulet comments on her husband's temper, telling him:
    You are too hot. ✪ How might the four actors stand on the
    stage at this moment in the action in order to show their
    relationships with each other?

5   (lines 187–207) Capulet is **calmer** now. He gives his point
     of view. He has worked very hard to find a good match for
     Juliet. He offers her a handsome man from a good family
     and she refuses. He cannot understand why. Capulet
     clearly regards Juliet as his property, to be done with as he
     wishes: *And you be mine, I'll give you to my friend.* Juliet's
     choice is simple – marry Paris or leave home, penniless.

JULIET IS ABANDONED BY LADY CAPULET AND THE NURSE

After her father leaves, Juliet appeals to her mother, asking her
to delay the marriage. Lady Capulet brushes Juliet off and
leaves. Why does she refuse to help? Juliet turns to the Nurse
and asks for comfort and advice. She expects to be helped by
her friend, who has always been on her side in the past. But
the Nurse advises Juliet to marry Paris and forget about
Romeo. ✪ Why do you think the Nurse does this?

Juliet cannot at first believe that the Nurse means what she is
saying. She asks her: *Speak'st thou from thy heart?* When the
Nurse replies yes, Juliet withdraws into herself. Look at her
words to the Nurse (lines 243–246). They are cold and ironic.
Only after the Nurse leaves does she say what she really
means. She curses the Nurse for what she has said and
declares that their close relationship is over. Betrayed by her
parents and her close friend, she turns to the only person
she has left, the Friar. If he cannot help, she will resort to
suicide.

Test yourself

Questions (answers on p. 57)
1   In Act 3, scene 4, what day does Lord Capulet arrange for
    the wedding?
2   What bird is really singing at the beginning of Act 3,
    scene 5? What time of day is it?
3   What has Lady Capulet come to tell Juliet in Act 3, scene 5?
4   What does Lord Capulet say he will do if Juliet does not
    marry Paris?

Assignments

? In Act 3, scene 5, there are many references to death that seem to foretell the eventual outcome of the play. For example: *I must be gone and live, or stay and die* (line 11). List and memorize at least three others.

? Look at Lord Capulet's words in Act 3, scene 5, lines 131–207. Choose one complete sentence from each of the five sections outlined on pages 54–56. Read each sentence aloud. What does each sentence tell you about Lord Capulet's feelings at that moment? How do the sentences differ from one another in language and sentence length?

? Juliet plays many parts in Act 3, scene 5: the teasing lover, the dutiful daughter, the disobedient daughter, the child in need of help. Find the lines in the scene where she is really herself, where she really means what she says.

Think about ...

In Act 1, scene 2, Capulet says that Juliet must agree to marry Paris before he will give his consent. In Act 3, scene 4, he arranges the wedding with Paris, and in Act 3, scene 5, he orders Juliet to marry. Why do you think he changes? And why is he in such a hurry for the wedding to take place?

Answers

1 Thursday.
2 The lark. Dawn.
3 That her father has arranged for her to marry Paris.
4 He will cast her out of his house without a penny (lines 200–207).

time is running out but it's time you took a break

Act 4 *scene* 1

◆ Paris visits Friar Lawrence to arrange wedding to Juliet.
◆ Juliet comes to see the Friar and meets Paris.
◆ The Friar thinks of a plan to help Juliet.

PARIS TALKS TO THE FRIAR

Paris tells the Friar that Lord Capulet has agreed to a wedding between Paris and Juliet on Thursday. ✪ Given that the Friar has already married Juliet to Romeo, how do you think he will respond to this news? Imagine how he might deliver lines 1, 4–5, and 16–17.

Look at the contrast between slowness and haste in this section. Juliet and the Friar would like to delay the marriage, but Paris is keen for it to take place as soon as possible.

THE CONFESSION AND THE PLAN

Juliet meets Paris on her way to see Friar Lawrence. The conversation between them is full of double meanings. Juliet is cool toward Paris, revealing nothing of her feelings. ✪ What do Paris' lines tell you of his feelings toward Juliet?

When Paris leaves, Juliet begs the Friar to help her. She says that if he cannot think of a plan, she will kill herself. The Friar stops her and asks her if she is brave enough to carry out his plan. ✪ What six courageous things does Juliet say she would rather do than marry Paris? The Friar outlines his plan to Juliet in lines 91–122. (Keywords to help you remember are in **bold type**.)

1   (lines 91–92) Juliet must go home and **agree to marry Paris** on Thursday.
2   (lines 93–94) On Wednesday night she must make sure that she **sleeps alone**.
3   (lines 95–106) Juliet must take a **potion** that makes her appear dead.
4   (lines 107–108) Juliet will **sleep for 42 hours**, then wake up.
5   (lines 109–114) Her family will place her in the **family vault**.
6   (lines 115–116) In the meantime, the Friar will **write to Romeo**, explaining the plan.
7   (lines 117–118) The Friar and Romeo will come to **get Juliet** when she **wakes up**.
8   (line 119) Romeo will take Juliet to **Mantua**.

Juliet agrees to the plan. ✪ What do you think of the Friar's plan? What could go wrong? Can you think of a better idea?

Act 4 *scene* 2

- ◆ The Capulet household prepares for the wedding.
- ◆ Juliet apologizes to her father.
- ◆ Lord Capulet moves the date of the wedding forward to Wednesday.

WEDDING PREPARATIONS

Capulet instructs the servants to get ready for the wedding. He asks one to hire *twenty cunning cooks*. Do you remember in Act 3, scene 4, when he told Paris there would be *no great ado* because of Tybalt's death? Now it seems as if the preparations are for a great feast.

JULIET ASKS FORGIVENESS

Juliet returns from confession and asks her father to forgive her. She promises always to do what he says in the future. Lord Capulet's immediate reaction is to move the wedding forward a day to Wednesday (line 25). Lady Capulet protests at the change of plan, saying that Thursday is soon enough and that they will not be ready in time for a wedding on Wednesday. But Lord Capulet overrules her. He seems very pleased with Juliet's change of heart and anxious to have the wedding as soon as possible. He bustles around, organizing everyone, enjoying the power he holds within the household.

Act 4 *scene* 3

- ◆ Juliet asks the Nurse and Lady Capulet to leave her alone.
- ◆ She fears what might happen to her after she has taken the potion.
- ◆ She drinks the potion and falls on the bed.

MOTHER AND NURSE

 Juliet asks both Lady Capulet and the Nurse to leave her alone. She sends them away together because, to her, they are part of the same problem. They represent the outside world that does not understand her love. Once the Nurse was Juliet's friend and confidante, now, Juliet treats her with the same cool formality as Lady Capulet. ✪ Do you think the Nurse notices this change? How might she feel about it if she does?

JULIET ALONE

Left alone, Juliet feels frightened. She almost calls the Nurse back, but realizes it would be pointless. Juliet prepares to take the potion, but first she considers what may happen after she drinks it. These are her fears. The **bold-type** keywords should help you to memorize them.

1   (lines 22–24) The mixture might **not work** at all. Juliet has a **dagger** as a safeguard; if it does not work, she can kill herself.

2   (lines 25–30) The Friar might have given Juliet a **real poison** in order to kill her, to avoid the dilemma of having to marry her to Paris when he has already married her to Romeo.

3   (lines 31–36) She might wake up in the tomb before Romeo comes and **suffocate** in the bad air.

4   (lines 37–58) Juliet might wake up in the tomb before Romeo comes and be **driven mad** by fear.

   Juliet's language becomes more and more uncontrolled during this speech. She does not pause for breath; this whole section is one sentence. Toward the end, Juliet works herself into a frenzy of fear (lines 51–54). The last few lines seem to indicate that she is hallucinating and can see Tybalt's ghost.

Juliet drinks the potion, calling out for Romeo as she does so.

Try to identify Juliet's fears

Test yourself

Questions (Answers below)

1 How many hours will Friar Lawrence's potion make Juliet sleep? When, approximately, will she wake up if she takes it the night before the (revised) wedding to Paris?

2 What does Juliet think might happen if she wakes in the tomb before Romeo arrives?

Assignments

? Draw a simple storyboard or Mind Map of Friar Lawrence's plan (Act 4, scene 1), or of Juliet's fears (Act 4, scene 2).

? Juliet's speech in Act 4, scene 3, is filled with horrific imagery. Imagine you are making a horror film based on Juliet's speech. Make a list of what you might need for this sequence. Include the following: actors, sets, props, costume, lighting, special effects, sound, and music.

Think about ...

? Look closely at Act 4, scene 1, lines 51–68. Compare Juliet's reaction to the planned wedding to Paris with Romeo's response to banishment in Act 3, scene 3. The Friar witnesses both. Both threaten to kill themselves. What are the similarities? What are the differences? What does the Friar think in each case?

Answers

1 42 hours. Thursday night.

2 She might suffocate (lines 31–36) or go mad (lines 37–58).

now take a break before a deadly discovery

Act 4 *scene* 4

◆ Preparations for the wedding feast continue.
◆ Music outside signals Paris's arrival.

GETTING READY

There are several scenes in the play that begin with the hustle and bustle of getting ready for a party (Act 1, scene 5; Act 4, scene 2; Act 4, scene 4). ❷ What do you think is the purpose of showing these preparations? How could you bring out their humor?

Lady Capulet implies that her husband is a womanizer: *you have been a mouse-hunt in your time.* ❷ What has just happened to make her say this? Do you think her lines (lines 12–13) are serious or playful?

PARIS ARRIVES

Lord Capulet jokes with the servants. He suddenly realizes that it is morning and Paris is arriving with music playing, as he said he would. Capulet sends the Nurse to wake Juliet, and goes to meet Paris.

Act 4 *scene* 5

◆ The Nurse comes to wake Juliet and finds her apparently dead.
◆ Lord and Lady Capulet come in and all three mourn.
◆ The Friar, Paris, and musicians arrive.
◆ The musicians joke with each other.

THE NURSE TRIES TO WAKE JULIET

The Nurse enters Juliet's bedroom calling and joking to her. She advises her to get as much sleep as she can now for Paris will not allow her much rest after they are married. The Nurse eventually realizes that she cannot rouse Juliet and thinks she is dead. The potion that Juliet took at the end of scene 3 has taken effect. The Nurse cries out and Lady Capulet comes in.

MOURNING

The language of the Nurse and Lady Capulet is similar in this scene. They seem to be united in their grief over Juliet's "death," and their language shows this. Both women repeat words and sounds (particularly "o"). They use short phrases and the lines of one mirror those of the other (see lines 23–24). The Nurse is an emotional character and we have heard her speaking like this several times, as, for example, when she returns to Juliet with news of Tybalt's death in Act 3, scene 2. Lady Capulet has only expressed emotion in this way once in the play – in Act 3, scene 1, when Tybalt was killed.

Lord Capulet reacts differently. His first lines (30–34) seem quite formal. How could an actor vary the way he delivers these lines to produce different meanings? Capulet goes on to say that he is unable to speak properly, that *Death ... ties up my tongue*. For the ordinarily very vocal Capulet this is quite an admission! It seems to indicate that he really is affected by grief.

THE WEDDING PARTY ARRIVE

Friar Lawrence, Paris, and the musicians enter. Capulet explains that Juliet is dead.

He uses an image of Death lying with Juliet on the night before her wedding to Paris. He repeats this image several times: *Death is my son-in-law, Death is my heir,/ My daughter hath he wedded*. Capulet believes that Juliet is dead and it is therefore true that Juliet has wedded Death. But Capulet's words also have another, hidden, meaning. He is unconsciously describing the true situation. Romeo is his son-in-law, Romeo is his heir, Romeo has wedded his daughter. Romeo could be described as Death for Juliet, because she will die because of him.

THE FRIAR'S ADVICE

Friar Lawrence interrupts to offer some religious consolation. He tells the mourners that Juliet is in heaven and that they should be glad for her. He asks the family to dress Juliet in her best clothes and take her to the church. The Friar knows that Juliet is not dead but he acts as if she were. ✪ What do you think is going through his mind during this scene?

THE MUSICIANS

Everyone leaves except the musicians. Peter, the Nurse's servant, comes in and teases them. ✪ Why do you think Shakespeare includes this lighthearted section at the end of the scene?

Test yourself

Questions (Answers below)
1   What do the following characters say when they find out Juliet is "dead": the Nurse, Lord Capulet, Lady Capulet?
2   What does Friar Lawrence tell the Capulet family to do with Juliet's body?
3   Which two songs are mentioned by Peter to the musicians? Why are they relevant to this scene?

Assignment
?   At the end of Act 4, scene 4, Capulet goes to have a "chat" with Paris. What do you think he will say? Script an imaginary scene where this takes place.

Think about ...
In Act 4, scene 5, Lady Capulet, the Nurse, Paris, and Lord Capulet all believe Juliet is dead. Look at lines 49, 55, 61, and 65. Notice that each line is spoken by a different character but the style is similar. What does each line tell you about the character who speaks it? What or who are they describing?

Answers
1   Nurse: *Alas, alas! Help, help! my lady's dead!*
    Lord Capulet: *Hah, let me see her. Out alas, she's cold,*
    Lady Capulet: *O me, O me, my child, my only life!*
2   Put rosemary on her corpse, dress her in her best clothes, and take her to church (lines 85–87)
3   "My heart is full" (lines 110–111) refers to the strong emotion felt by Peter at the "death" of Juliet. He asks the musicians to play "Heart's ease" (lines 106–108) in the hope that it will make him feel better.

take a break before the tragic ending

Act 5   *scene* 1

◆ Romeo talks about his dream.
◆ Balthasar arrives with news of Juliet's "death."
◆ Romeo decides to kill himself in the tomb with Juliet.
◆ Romeo buys some poison from an apothecary.

GOOD DREAMS, BAD NEWS

Romeo talks about his dream in which Juliet came and found him dead but she kissed him and breathed life back into him. Ironically, this dream will come true, but without the happy ending. Juliet will wake in the tomb to find Romeo dead. Realizing that he has killed himself with poison, she will kiss him in the hope of tasting a few drops and killing herself.

Balthasar arrives and Romeo asks him what news he has brought from Verona. He asks if the Friar has sent any letters. Romeo will ask Balthasar this question again in line 33. Unfortunately, the Friar did not send his letter with Balthasar, but with Friar John. If Balthasar had brought the Friar's letter to Romeo now, things could have turned out very differently; Romeo would have realized that Juliet was not really dead. As it is, Balthasar brings him the news that everyone else in Verona believes to be true – Juliet is dead and lies in the Capulet tomb.

ROMEO'S REACTION

Romeo's immediate reaction to the news is *Is it e'en so?* *then I defy you stars!* ✪ What do you think Romeo is feeling at this moment? How could an actor deliver this line to express Romeo's emotion? Romeo tells Balthasar to go and arrange for horses for them to return to Verona. Balthasar is worried about Romeo. What does he think he might do?

THE APOTHECARY'S SHOP

Romeo decides to kill himself in the tomb with Juliet. In lines 52–57, he remembers seeing a poor apothecary (chemist) in Mantua and thinking that he looked as if he might sell poison, despite its being illegal. ✪ Why do you think Romeo had this forethought? While Romeo is talking, he is walking through the streets, looking for the apothecary's shop. Eventually, he finds it (line 58).

The shop is closed because of a holiday but Romeo calls the apothecary out. Romeo explains that he wants to buy a deadly poison and offers a large sum of money. The apothecary is reluctant but he needs the money badly and so he agrees. He gives Romeo the poison and Romeo gives him the money. Romeo remarks that it is money that is the real poison, causing more death than the apothecary's mixtures.

Other references to money in the play are linked with marriage. The Nurse and Lady Capulet urge Juliet to marry Paris because she will gain wealth. It is implied that Lady Capulet married for money when she was very young.

Act 5 *scene* 2

◆ Friar John returns with Friar Lawrence's letter to Romeo. He has been unable to deliver it.
◆ Friar Lawrence sets off for the Capulet tomb.

"UNHAPPY FORTUNE!"

It seems that every time the Friar thinks of a plan to help Romeo and Juliet, fate intervenes to spoil it. At the end of Act 4, scene 1, the Friar told Juliet that he would write to Romeo explaining the plan to pretend that Juliet is dead, and asking Romeo to come and get her. He said that he would send this letter to Mantua with another friar. Now Friar John, the man he sent, returns and tells him that this important letter has not been delivered.

WHY WAS THE LETTER NOT DELIVERED?

After Friar Lawrence gave him the letter, Friar John went to look for another friar to go with him to Mantua. He found his friend visiting the house of a sick person. Unfortunately, before they could leave, the *searchers* (city health officers) declared the house a plague area and sealed up the doors, refusing to allow anyone to enter or leave. Friar John has been stuck there ever since.

FRIAR LAWRENCE'S REACTION

Friar Lawrence fears that the nondelivery of his letter *may do much danger.* ❂ What do you think he is worrying about? The Friar sends for a crowbar and sets off for the Capulet tomb. He plans to bring Juliet back to his cell and write again to Romeo, asking him to come and get her.

Act 5 *scene* 3

◆ Paris comes to pay his respects at the Capulet tomb.
◆ Romeo arrives, fights with Paris, and kills him.
◆ Romeo enters tomb and finds Juliet. He drinks the poison.
◆ The Friar arrives.
◆ Juliet wakes. The Friar tells her Romeo is dead and tries to persuade her to leave. Juliet refuses and the Friar runs away.
◆ Juliet stabs herself with Romeo's dagger.
◆ The Watch (Watchmen) arrive and call the Prince, the Capulets, and the Montagues.
◆ The Friar explains what has happened.
◆ The Prince blames the feud.
◆ Montague and Capulet shake hands and agree to erect a gold statue of their children.

Paris in Mourning

Paris enters the churchyard and asks his page to listen for anyone coming near. He says *I would not be seen.* Why do you think Paris wants to keep his visit to Juliet's tomb a secret? Paris sprinkles flowers and perfumed water around the tomb. His page whistles to him, signaling that someone is coming. Paris hides to see who it is.

Romeo and Balthasar

Romeo approaches the tomb. He asks Balthasar for a pickax and a crowbar to help him force his way into the tomb, gives him a letter to deliver to Lord Montague, then asks him to leave. Romeo tells Balthasar that he is going into the tomb for two reasons: to see Juliet's face and to retrieve a ring from her finger. Romeo threatens to kill Balthasar if he spies on him. Balthasar agrees to go and Romeo gives him a purse full of money. But Balthasar decides to stay. ✪ What does he think Romeo will do? Why do you think he decides to stay after Romeo has threatened him?

Paris challenges Romeo

As Romeo tries to enter the tomb, Paris challenges him. Paris recognizes Romeo as Tybalt's murderer. He also believes that Juliet died because of her grief over Tybalt. He suspects that Romeo intends to defile the Capulet tomb. For Paris it is a point of honor to stop Romeo from entering the tomb. Paris tells Romeo that he must die (remember that his sentence was banishment and death if he should return to Verona).

Romeo urges Paris to leave him alone, hinting that he intends to kill himself anyway, but his riddles confuse Paris, who tries to arrest Romeo. Compare Romeo's words here (lines 58–67) with the words he spoke to Tybalt in Act 3, scene 1, lines 69–73. In both cases Romeo tries to make peace, and in both instances he is misunderstood. They fight and Romeo kills Paris. Paris's page sees them fighting and goes to call the Watch.

ROMEO'S LAST SPEECH

Romeo is confused. He seems to remember Balthasar telling him that Paris and Juliet were to be married, but he is not sure. Despite this, Romeo speaks to Paris as if he were a friend and grants Paris's dying wish to be laid alongside Juliet. ❂ Why do you think he does this? The inside of the Capulet tomb must have been small, cold, damp, and dark, but Romeo says that Juliet's beauty transforms the tomb into a *feasting presence full of light*. Romeo talks to Juliet, telling her that Death has not taken away her beauty, and that her lips and cheeks still look red. This is ironic – she looks alive because she is not dead; in fact, she is about to wake up in a few minutes. Romeo sees Tybalt's body and asks his forgiveness, promising Tybalt to kill the person who murdered him, by killing himself.

Romeo imagines that Death is keeping Juliet as his lover. This idea reminds us of Capulet's speech when Juliet is found "dead." He, too, describes Death as her lover (Act 4, scene 5, lines 40–46). Romeo promises to stay with her to protect her from Death. He sees his own death as releasing him from the bad luck (*inauspicious stars*) that has plagued his life.

Romeo's final farewell to Juliet focuses on his *eyes, arms,* and *lips.* He says good-bye to Juliet in the physical world in order to join her beyond death. He turns to his poison, addressing it as *bitter conduct* and *unsavory guide*, contrasting the bad taste of the drug with the good effect it will have in guiding him to Juliet.

Romeo says good-bye to Juliet; what happens next?

These last few lines use an image of life as a sea journey, reminding us of Romeo's words before meeting Juliet at the party (Act 1, scene 5) and Capulet's words to Juliet before their argument (Act 3, scene 5, lines 131–143). Romeo takes the poison and dies instantly.

THE FRIAR COMES TO GET JULIET

The Friar's first words are a complete change for him. Throughout the play he has been advising slowness and caution. Now he asks for speed and stumbles over graves in his haste. ❂ What has happened to change him?

When Balthasar tells him that Romeo is in the tomb, the Friar fears the worst and rushes in. He finds Romeo and Paris dead and Juliet awakening. Juliet asks the Friar where Romeo is. The Friar tells Juliet that Romeo is dead and asks her to come away with him. He offers to *dispose* of her to *a sisterhood of holy nuns.*

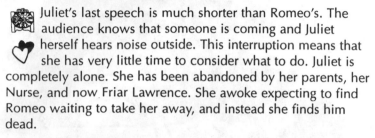

The Friar is clearly afraid of being caught. He tells Juliet, *I dare no longer stay.* ✪ Do you think the Friar is right to leave Juliet in the tomb? Remember that, in the end, the Friar's involvement is discovered and the Prince pardons him.

JULIET'S LAST SPEECH

Juliet's last speech is much shorter than Romeo's. The audience knows that someone is coming and Juliet herself hears noise outside. This interruption means that she has very little time to consider what to do. Juliet is completely alone. She has been abandoned by her parents, her Nurse, and now Friar Lawrence. She awoke expecting to find Romeo waiting to take her away, and instead she finds him dead.

She refuses to leave with the Friar and turns to Romeo. She finds that he has killed himself with poison. Her words tell us that she tries to drink a few remaining drops from the cup and from Romeo's lips in order that she may die as well. Notice how Juliet talks about the poison as if it were a good thing (*friendly drop, restorative*) that will take her to Romeo.

There is no more poison in the cup or on Romeo's lips, but she remarks that his lips are warm. This is especially tragic as it shows her that it is not long since Romeo died. At this point, Juliet hears someone approaching. She has no time to ask questions or to be afraid. She takes Romeo's dagger, and with a few short words, stabs herself.

THE WATCH ARRIVE

Paris's page brings the Watch to the tomb. The Captain instructs his men to search the churchyard and bring back anyone they find. The Captain finds Paris dead and Juliet *bleeding, warm, and newly dead.* This must strike him as mysterious as she has *lain this two days buried.* The Captain sends for the Prince, the Montagues, and the Capulets. The Watchmen find the Friar and Balthasar in the churchyard and bring them back to the tomb.

REACTIONS TO THE TRAGEDY

The Prince and the Capulets arrive at the tomb. The Captain explains what has happened. Lord and Lady Capulet see Juliet, newly dead, and suffer the agony of losing their daughter for a second time. Lord Montague enters and explains that his wife has died of grief over Romeo's exile. He now has to face the loss of his son as well.

Look at the reactions of Lord Capulet (lines 210–213) and Lord Montague (lines 222–223). Each remarks on how something is out of place. Capulet says that the dagger has made a mistake – it should be in its sheath on Romeo's back and instead it is in Juliet's bosom. Montague criticizes Romeo for bad manners, for pushing in front of his father into his grave. Both these comments reflect the idea that the natural order of things has been upset by the deaths of Romeo and Juliet.

TIME FOR EXPLANATIONS

The Prince asks for an explanation and the Friar offers his version of events. His speech (lines 238-278), though long, is clear and direct. The language is simple, there is no unnecessary description, and the Friar does not spend time talking about his own reasons for acting as he did. He explains what happened and invites the Prince to punish him. The Prince forgives him. ✪ If you were the Prince, what would you do?

Next, Balthasar explains what Romeo did. The Prince takes the letter that Romeo wrote to his father. ✪ How do you think Lord Montague feels while the Prince is reading this letter? Paris's page explains how his master was involved.

After reading the letter, the Prince announces that it confirms what the Friar has said. He blames the feud between the Capulets and Montagues for causing the tragedy. He also blames himself for allowing the feud to continue.

RECONCILIATION

Capulet calls Montague *brother* and offers to shake his hand. Montague offers to build a gold statue of Juliet and Capulet says he will build one of Romeo by her side.

Test yourself

Questions (Answers opposite)

1   What does Romeo buy in Act 5, scene 1?
2   Why did Romeo not receive Friar Lawrence's letter explaining the plan to pretend Juliet was dead?
3   Is it day or night at the beginning of Act 5, scene 3? How do you know?
4   Both Paris and Romeo give their servants instructions in Act 5, scene 3. What does Paris ask his page to do? What does Romeo ask Balthasar to do?
5   In Act 5, scene 3, who alerts the Watch? Who is captured by the Watch?
6   The Prince says he has lost a *brace of kinsmen*. How many has he lost? Who are they?

Assignments

?   At the beginning of Act 5, scene 3, Romeo gives Balthasar a letter to deliver to his father. At the end of the scene, the Prince reads the letter. We are never told exactly what the letter says. Write Romeo's letter to his father, explaining the events of the past five days.

?   Look at Romeo's last speech (Act 5, scene 3, lines 74–120). He addresses several different people. Read each line aloud and decide who it is addressed to. What do you think Romeo is doing at each stage of this speech?

?   The Friar's speech (Act 5, scene 3, lines 238–278) is a useful summary of the events in the play. Read the speech aloud. For each line, choose keywords and write them down. For example, the first keyword might be **brief**.

Think about ...

The Prince says, *Some shall be pardoned, and some punished* (Act 5, scene 3, line 329). Who do you think should be pardoned? Who should be punished? What should their punishment be?

Answers

1   A poison to kill himself.

2   Friar Lawrence gave the letter to Friar John to deliver to Mantua. Unfortunately, Friar John became trapped in a house that had been sealed up as a plague area.

3   Night. Paris brings a *torch* (line 1). He says he will visit the tomb *nightly* (line 17) and, when he hides from Romeo, he says *Muffle me, night* (line 21).

4   Paris asks his page to: give him a torch; stand at a distance; listen to the ground so that he will know by the vibration if anyone is coming; whistle if he hears anything. Romeo asks Balthasar to: give him a mattock (digging tool) and wrenching iron, deliver a letter to his father, give him a light, stand at a distance, and not interfere with anything Romeo does.

5   Paris's page alerts the Watch. The Friar and Balthasar are found in the churchyard and brought back to the tomb.

6   Two. Mercutio and Paris.

now that you've reached the end of the play, take a well-earned break

TOPICS FOR DISCUSSION AND BRAINSTORMING

One of the best ways to review is with one or more friends. Even if you're with someone who hardly knows the text you're studying, you'll find that having to explain things to your friend will help you to organize your own thoughts and memorize key points. If you're with someone who has studied the text, you'll find that the things you can't remember are different from the things your friend can't remember, so you'll be able to help each other.

Discussion will also help you to develop interesting new ideas that perhaps neither of you would have had alone. Use a **brainstorming** approach to tackle any of the topics listed below. Allow yourself to share whatever ideas come into your head, however meaningless they seem. This will get you thinking creatively.

Whether alone or with a friend, use Mind Mapping (see p. vi) to help you brainstorm and organize your ideas. If you are with a friend, use a large sheet of paper and thick colored pens.

Any of the topics below could appear on an exam, but be sure to answer the precise question given.

TOPICS

? Look at Act 1, scene 3. Compare Lady Capulet's words with those of the Nurse. Read the words aloud, thinking about these questions. What does each woman talk about? What do you notice about the way you read the lines of Lady Capulet and the Nurse? Is there any difference in your tone of voice, the speed in which you read, how loudly you speak? What does their language tell you about their characters? Both Lady Capulet and the Nurse think it is a good idea for Juliet to marry Paris. What reasons do you think each of them would give for this?

? What do the following scenes in the play tell you about Lord Capulet's feelings for Tybalt: Act 1, scene 5; Act 3, scene 1; and Act 3, scene 4?

? Is the play more about love or hate?

? Romeo and Juliet seem to meet in a quiet and intimate setting, removed from the main action of the Capulet party. If you were directing the play, how would you stage this scene? Think about these questions: How do the actors enter at the beginning of the scene? How do Romeo and his friends get into the party? Where does Romeo first see Juliet? Where is Tybalt when he hears Romeo? Where do Romeo and Juliet meet? How does Capulet deal with Tybalt's anger without letting his guests know that something is wrong?

? Friar Lawrence warns Romeo in Act 2, scene 3, *Wisely and slow, they stumble that run fast.* Do you think that the tragic events later in the play could have been avoided if Romeo had taken this advice?

? Act 2, scene 5, contrasts Juliet's youth and impatience with the Nurse's age and weariness. How could actors playing this scene show this contrast through their movements and body language?

? At the beginning of Act 3, scene 3, Friar Lawrence tells Romeo that *Affliction is enamoured of thy part,/ And thou art wedded to calamity.* Is it true that Romeo is jinxed? Where in the play is Romeo's future linked to fate or fortune? Could Romeo have escaped his tragic end?

? Compare Romeo's language in the scene where he first meets Juliet (Act 1, scene 5) and the scene in which they part (Act 3, scene 5). Has his language changed? If so, how? What does this tell you about Romeo's relationship with Juliet?

? Why did Friar Lawrence try to help Romeo and Juliet? Look back through the play and try to find evidence that backs up your opinion. Look at Act 2, scene 3; Act 3, scene 3; and Act 4, scene 1.

? Look at the final speeches of Romeo (Act 5, scene 3, lines 75–120) and Juliet (Act 5, scene 3, lines 165–175). How do they confirm what you already know or think about their characters? Do these final words alter your opinions in any way?

HOW TO GET AN "A" IN ENGLISH LITERATURE

In all your study, in coursework, and in exams, be aware of the following:

- **Characterization** – the characters and what we know about them (what they say and do, how the author describes them), their relationships, and how they develop.
- **Plot and structure** – what happens and how the plot is organized into parts or episodes.
- **Setting and atmosphere** – the changing scene and how it reflects the story (for example, a rugged landscape and storm reflecting a character's emotional difficulties).
- **Style and language** – the author's choice of words, and literary devices such as imagery, and how these reflect the mood.
- **Viewpoint** – how the story is told (for example, through an imaginary narrator, or in the third person but through the eyes of one character – "She was furious – how dare he!").
- **Social and historical context** – influences on the author (see Background in this guide).

Develop your ability to:

- Relate **detail** to **broader content, meaning, and style**.
- Show understanding of the author's **intentions, technique, and meaning** (brief and appropriate comparisons with other works by the same author will earn credit).
- Give **personal response and interpretation**, backed up by **examples** and short **quotations**.
- **Evaluate** the author's achievement (how completely does the author succeed and why?)

THE EXAM ESSAY

PLANNING

A literary essay of about 250 to 400 words on a theme from *Romeo and Juliet* will challenge your skills as an essay writer. It is worth taking some time to plan your essay carefully. An excellent way to do this is in the three stages below:

1 Make a **Mind Map** of your ideas on the theme suggested. Brainstorm and write down any ideas that pop into your head.
2 Taking ideas from your Mind Map, **organize** them into an outline choosing a logical sequence of information. Choose significant details and quotations to support your main thesis.
3 Be sure you have both a strong **opening paragraph** stating your main idea and giving the title and author of the literary work you will be discussing, and a **conclusion** that sums up your main points.

WRITING AND EDITING

Write your essay carefully, allowing at least five minutes at the end to check for errors of fact as well as for correct spelling, grammar, and punctuation.

REMEMBER!

Stick to the thesis you are trying to support and avoid unnecessary plot summary. Always support your ideas with relevant details and quotations from the text.

MODEL ANSWER AND PLAN

The next (and final) chapter consists of a model essay on a theme from *Romeo and Juliet* followed by a Mind Map and an essay plan used to write it. Use these to get an idea of how an essay about *Romeo and Juliet* might be organized and how to break up your information into a logical sequence of paragraphs.

Before reading the answer, you might like to do a plan of your own, then compare it with the example. The numbered points with comments at the end, show why it's a good answer.

QUESTION

Many works of literature show the growth and development of a young person. Discuss how Romeo, from William Shakespeare's tragedy *Romeo and Juliet,* changes during the course of the play.

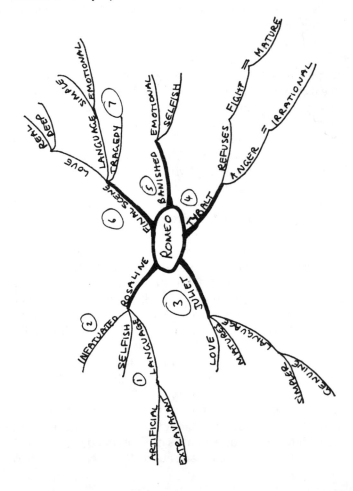

PLAN

1 **Introduction.** Gives setting, title, and author of work discussed. Some historical background. Feud.
Body Paragraphs
2 Romeo's infatuation with Rosaline. Elaborate, artificial language. His parents' attitude.
3 Meets Juliet. Language begins to change. Romeo feels real emotion. Marriage and love.
4 Banishment and final scene. Depth and importance of Romeo's love.
5 **Conclusion.** Romeo matures during course of the play. Tragedy. Romeo did not take an active role in the feud and yet is destroyed by it.

ESSAY

The growth and development of a young person is often the subject of works of literature. This is particularly true of William Shakespeare's tragedy *Romeo and Juliet* in which a young man is changed very quickly by the power of love from a callow and immature youth into a young man capable of genuine and strong emotion. Shakespeare's play is set in Renaissance Verona where two families, the Capulets and the Montagues, have long been involved in a bitter feud.

When Romeo, the son of Lord Montague, is first introduced in Act I, scene 1, he is presented as a youth so totally involved in his unrequited love for a young woman named Rosaline that he seems aware of nothing else. His language is so extravagant and full of poetic devices that the audience wonders whether he is more in love with the *idea* of being in love than someone in the thrall of real feeling. He speaks in riddles, using oxymorons to reflect his confused state of mind: "Feather of lead, bright smoke, cold fire, sick health,/ Still-waking sleep, that is not what is!" His friend Benvolio tries to cheer him up, and, to take his mind off Rosaline, eventually persuades Romeo to gate-crash a party they hear about that will be held at the Capulet's house.

It is at this party, at the home of the Montagues' bitter enemies, that Romeo, unaware of her identity, see and falls in love with Juliet. He uses images of light and dark to describe her beauty: "It seems she hangs upon the cheek of night/ As a rich jewel in an Ethiop's ear." Romeo and Juliet are immediately attracted to one another and speak in almost religious terms. Romeo says, "If I profane with my unworthiest hand/ This holy shrine...." He already seems changes and shows real emotion, which is evident when he later realizes Juliet's identity. Romeo risks death when he climbs into the Capulet's orchard later that night, which can be seen both as the rash impetuous act of a thoughtless young man but also the brave act of someone truly in love.

After Romeo and Juliet's secret marriage, Romeo shows increased maturity in Act 3, scene 1, when he refuses to fight Tybalt, Juliet's "fiery" cousin since he is now related to Tybalt by marriage. When Romeo tries to stop Mercutio and Tybalt from fighting, he shows his awareness of the Prince's edict against public brawling; however, Romeo's rational behavior ends when Mercutio is killed and, overcome with rage and guilt, he kills Tybalt. Romeo is devastated by the thought of his banishment: "There is no world without Verona's walls,/ But purgatory, torture, hell itself."

After spending the night with Juliet, Romeo is more optimistic and sensible and realizes that he must leave Verona but plans to contact Juliet whenever he can. Fate intervenes in the form of Friar Lawrence's botched plans and, in the final scene of the play, when he finds Juliet apparently dead, his final speech is strong and full of love, lacking the artifice of his language in the first act of the play. His suicide is not the rash act of an immature young man but because he loves Juliet more than life itself: "O my love, my wife,/ Death, that has sucked the honey of thy breath,/ Hath no power yet upon thy beauty." He dies because he loves Juliet and is not willing to live his life without her.

Thus, although Romeo is often rash and emotional, he does show maturity in his love for Juliet, and his shallow infatuation with Rosaline at the beginning of the play is replaced with a mature and sincere love for Juliet. The tragedy of the play is that a feud, which has nothing to do with Romeo and Juliet personally, destroys both their lives just at the point when Romeo was beginning to grow and mature.

WHAT'S SO GOOD ABOUT IT?

1 Strong opening paragragh.
2 Gives title, author, setting, and theme.
3 Good understanding of plot.
4 Awareness of literary devices.
5 Good use of quotations from text.
6 Awareness of character development.
7 Good organization into paragraphs.
8 Good grasp of spelling, grammar, and vocabulary.
9 Avoids plot summary.
10 Shows excellent understanding of Romeo's character.
11 Shows how the feud destroys lives.
12 Logical sequence of paragraphs.
13 Excellent supporting details.
14 Strong conclusion summing up main theme of essay.

GLOSSARY OF LITERARY TERMS

alliteration   repetition of a sound at the beginnings of words; for example, *ladies' lips.*

aside   a short speech spoken by one character, as if thinking aloud; not meant to be heard by others on stage.

blank verse   the kind of nonrhyming verse in which Shakespeare usually writes, with five pairs of syllables to each line, with the stress always on the second syllable; unrhymed iambic pentameter.

Chorus   traditionally, a group of actors (but often just one) used to introduce a play, summarize the plot, or comment on the action.

context   the social and historical influences on the author.

couplet   *see* rhyming couplet.

dramatic irony   *see* irony (dramatic)

foreshadowing   an indirect warning of things to come, often through imagery.

iambic pentameter   verse with five pairs of syllables to a line, with the stress always on the second syllable.

image   a word picture used to make an idea come alive, as in a **metaphor, simile,** or **personification** (see separate entries).

imagery   the kind of word picture used to make an idea come alive.

irony   (dramatic) where at least one character on stage is unaware of an important fact that the audience knows about, and that is somehow hinted at; **(simple)** ridiculing an opinion or belief by pretending to hold it, or pretending to be ignorant of the true facts, usually to show scorn or ridicule.

metaphor   a description of a thing as if it were something essentially different but also in some way similar; for example, describing love as *a smoke made with the fume of sighs*.

metrical foot   a number of syllables making up one beat in a verse style's meter.

oxymoron   poetic use of opposites to express paradox, as in *feather of lead*.

personification   a description of something as if it were a person.

prose   language in which, unlike verse, there is no set number of syllables in a line, and no rhyming.

pun   use of a word with two meanings, or of two similar-sounding words, where both meanings are appropriate in different ways.

rhyming couplet   a pair of rhyming lines, often used at the end of a speech.

setting   the place in which the action occurs, usually affecting the atmosphere; for example, the Capulet family vault.

simile   a comparison of two things that are different in most ways but similar in one important way, as in, *It seems she hangs upon the cheek of night/As a rich jewel in an Ethiop's ear.*

sonnet   a poem with 14 lines, broken into three sections: the first eight lines, rhyming ABABCDCD; the next four lines, rhyming EFEF, and a rhyming couplet at the end, rhyming GG; written in iambic pentameter (*see* blank verse).

structure   the organization of the plot.

theme   an idea explored by an author; conflict, for example.

tragedy   a play focusing on a tragic hero (see separate entry)

tragic hero   a character whose nobility or achievement we admire, and whose downfall and death through a weakness or error, coupled with fate, arouses our sympathy.

viewpoint   how the story is told – through action, or in discussion between minor characters, for instance.

INDEX